"At the time of the Reformatic
of the Lord's Supper than on a
be resolved, so what is a Christ
ment? This concise book by G.
discussion of the Supper squarely in the context of the Bible's teaching about covenants, providing a particularly helpful introduction to the nature of covenant meals."

Keith A. Mathison, Professor of Systematic Theology, Reformation
Bible College; author, *From Age to Age*; *Given for You*; and *The Shape
of Sola Scriptura*

"Many Christians suffer from a spiritual depth-perception problem or theological
myopia when they come to the Lord's Supper: all they see is bread and wine. Enter
Guy Waters, expert spiritual ophthalmologist. In a single consultation he restores our
depth perception and reduces our myopia. Perhaps to our surprise, he takes two-
thirds of his time patiently guiding us through the pages of the Old Testament. Surely
the Lord's Supper is a *new* covenant ordinance! But Waters knows what he is doing.
Prescribing biblically crafted lenses for us, he shows us the bread and wine again and
asks, 'Do you see more clearly now?' Read these pages carefully and you will find
yourself saying, 'Yes, it's so much clearer now. Thank you so much; it's wonderful!'"

Sinclair B. Ferguson, Chancellor's Professor of Systematic Theology,
Reformed Theological Seminary; Teaching Fellow, Ligonier Ministries

"In a warm and readable style, Guy Waters blesses the church again. By first
taking us on an engaging tour of the Bible's covenants, he sets the table for his
central concern—that in the communion meal the people of God 'truly dine
with our covenant Head,' the Lord Jesus Christ. From beginning to end, the
reader will find biblical texts surveyed persuasively, historic theological distinc-
tions tackled thoughtfully, and practical concerns addressed winsomely. Before
you next partake of the Lord's Supper, consume this volume first."

David B. Garner, Vice President for Advancement and Associate
Professor of Systematic Theology, Westminster Theological Seminary;
author, *Sons in the Son* and *How Can I Know for Sure?*

"Don't let this volume's slim size trick you. In it Guy Waters dispenses a wealth of
biblical reflection. Noting the Bible's covenantal structure and paying attention to
the entire biblical canon, he places the Supper of our Lord as the fulfillment of the
pattern of God's condescending to be present with his people and to give them signs
of his presence. You may not agree with all of Waters's conclusions. But everyone
will benefit from his engagement with the biblical text and his pastoral reflections
on the importance of the Supper for individual believers and the gathered church."

Shawn D. Wright, Professor of Church History, The Southern Baptist
Theological Seminary

"In this accessible, biblical-theological approach to the Lord's Supper, Waters demonstrates the Supper's integral place in redemptive history and its consequent importance for the life of the church, inasmuch as Christ offers himself as spiritual nourishment to be received through faith. This message needs to be heard and heeded. I hope this book has a wide readership."

> **Robert Letham,** Professor of Systematic and Historical Theology, Union School of Theology; author, *The Holy Trinity*; *Union with Christ*; and *The Work of Christ*

*The Lord's Supper as the Sign and
Meal of the New Covenant*

The Lord's Supper as the Sign and Meal of the New Covenant

Guy Prentiss Waters

CROSSWAY®
WHEATON, ILLINOIS

The Lord's Supper as the Sign and Meal of the New Covenant

Copyright © 2019 by Guy Prentiss Waters

Published by Crossway
    1300 Crescent Street
    Wheaton, Illinois 60187

Cover design: Jordan Singer

First printing 2019

Printed in the United States of America

Trade paperback ISBN: 978-1-4335-5837-5
ePub ISBN: 978-1-4335-5840-5
PDF ISBN: 978-1-4335-5838-2
Mobipocket ISBN: 978-1-4335-5839-9

Library of Congress Cataloging-in-Publication Data

Names: Waters, Guy Prentiss, 1975– author.
Title: The Lord's Supper as the sign and meal of the New Covenant / Guy Prentiss Waters.
Description: Wheaton, Illinois: Crossway, 2019. | Series: Short studies in biblical theology | Includes bibliographical references and index.
Identifiers: LCCN 2018017145 (print) | LCCN 2018044644 (ebook) | ISBN 9781433558382 (pdf) | ISBN 9781433558399 (mobi) | ISBN 9781433558405 (epub) | ISBN 9781433558375 (tp) | ISBN 9781433558405 (ePub) | ISBN 9781433558399 (Mobipocket)
Subjects: LCSH: Lord's Supper—Biblical teaching. | Covenant theology—Biblical teaching. | Christian life.
Classification: LCC BS2545.L58 (ebook) | LCC BS2545.L58 W38 2019 (print) | DDC 234/.163—dc23
LC record available at https://lccn.loc.gov/2018017145

Crossway is a publishing ministry of Good News Publishers.

BP			29	28	27	26	25	24	23	22	21	20	19
15	14	13	12	11	10	9	8	7	6	5	4	3	2	1

To my wife, Sarah,
fellow heir of the grace of life

Contents

Series Preface

Most of us tend to approach the Bible early on in our Christian lives as a vast, cavernous, and largely impenetrable book. We read the text piecemeal, finding golden nuggets of inspiration here and there, but remain unable to plug any given text meaningfully into the overarching storyline. Yet one of the great advances in evangelical biblical scholarship over the past few generations has been the recovery of biblical theology—that is, a renewed appreciation for the Bible as a theologically unified, historically rooted, progressively unfolding, and ultimately Christ-centered narrative of God's covenantal work in our world to redeem sinful humanity.

This renaissance of biblical theology is a blessing, yet little of it has been made available to the general Christian population. The purpose of Short Studies in Biblical Theology is to connect the resurgence of biblical theology at the academic level with everyday believers. Each volume is written by a capable scholar or churchman who is consciously writing in a way that requires no prerequisite theological training of the reader. Instead, any thoughtful Christian disciple can track with and benefit from these books.

Each volume in this series takes a whole-Bible theme and traces it through Scripture. In this way readers not only learn about a given theme but also are given a model for how to read the Bible as a coherent whole.

We have launched this series because we love the Bible, we love the church, and we long for the renewal of biblical theology in the academy to enliven the hearts and minds of Christ's disciples all around the world. As editors, we have found few discoveries more thrilling in life than that of seeing the whole Bible as a unified story of God's gracious acts of redemption, and indeed of seeing the whole Bible as ultimately about Jesus, as he himself testified (Luke 24:27; John 5:39).

The ultimate goal of Short Studies in Biblical Theology is to magnify the Savior and to build up his church—magnifying the Savior through showing how the whole Bible points to him and his gracious rescue of helpless sinners; and building up the church by strengthening believers in their grasp of these life-giving truths.

Dane C. Ortlund and Miles V. Van Pelt

Introduction

It is fair to say that many believers think of the Lord's Supper as a matter of long-standing controversy in the Christian church. What exactly happens at the Lord's Supper? What is the relationship between the body and blood of Jesus Christ and the bread and wine? How often should we observe the Lord's Supper? May we observe the Supper outside of the local church? What qualifies a person to come to the Lord's Table?

These questions touch on differences that have emerged within the Christian church concerning the doctrine and practice of the Lord's Supper. They are legitimate questions in themselves. To mention them as I have is not to say that they have no biblical answers. They do have answers. It is, rather, to observe that such questions may well tempt believers to retreat from the Lord's Supper. Christians might conclude that the Supper is a complex matter best taken up by seasoned theologians, that it is a matter of doctrinal controversy but of little practical importance. For all intents and purposes, they could reason, the Lord's Supper is best left to others; it has no meaningful significance to the Christian life.

It would be sad were Christians to come to such a conclusion. That would upend the whole purpose of God in giving the Lord's Supper to his people. That purpose is to support and strengthen the faith of believers. To deprive ourselves of the Supper is to deprive ourselves of the strength and assurance that God gives to our faith through it. One reason I have written this book is to help Christians recover the importance of the Lord's Supper in the Christian life through a renewed appreciation of the Supper as both a *sign* and the *meal* of the new covenant. Our aim is to see better how the Lord's Supper points to and confirms the blessings and benefits that God has poured out upon his people in Jesus Christ.

God's provision of the Supper is part of a long-standing pattern of his gracious dealings with his people throughout history. Just as God has always made covenants with his people, so also God has always given covenant *signs* and covenant *meals* to his people. In all of God's covenants, he has given his people tangible signs or tokens tied to the promises that he has made with them. God has also appointed meals for his covenant people to help them appreciate his goodness and abundance in the gospel. God appeals to us through our five senses—sight, hearing, touch, taste, and smell—to encourage us to believe the good news that he offers us in the promises of the gospel.

God has never chosen at random the physical elements that have made up the signs he appointed for his covenants, and it is no accident that he has appointed meals throughout redemptive history for his people. These signs and meals always have had some meaningful connection to the promises to which they correspond. There is a reason that in the Lord's Supper we partake of *bread* and *wine* at a *Table* that Christ has spread for us and to which he invites us.

If there is meaning and purpose to the signs and meals that God has appointed within his covenants, there is equally meaning and purpose to the covenants themselves. In other words, the covenants that God made with his people were not sporadic or disassociated events in the history of God's dealings with humanity. On the contrary, there is a glorious unity to the covenants of the Bible. When we grasp that unity, we will better appreciate the meaning of the signs and meals that God has given, along with the covenants he has made with his people. A full appreciation of the importance of the Lord's Supper in the Christian life requires us to look first to the progression of God's covenants in human history and then to the signs and meals that God appoints within those covenants.

The project we are undertaking goes by the name *biblical theology*. What is biblical theology? It is not simply theology that is true to the Bible. Biblical theology *is* that, but that definition covers many other things as well. A clear understanding of biblical theology will guide our reflections on the Lord's Supper.

Biblical theology must begin, as does any legitimate approach to the Bible, with the conviction that the Bible is the Word of God. The Bible is, in other words, the verbal revelation of God to humanity. For all the diversity represented in the Bible—different types of literature, different human authors, different primary audiences—the Bible has a single, divine author. That author has spoken, and his speech is the words and propositions that make up the books of the Old and New Testaments.

The chief concern of the Bible and, therefore, of the Bible's divine author, is salvation. The Bible assumes that all human beings (except one man, Jesus Christ) are sinners in need of salvation. God created man upright, but we, in Adam and by reason of our own sins, have gone astray. The Bible tells us what God has done so that sinners may be saved.

God's saving words and deeds did not transpire all at once. God gradually and progressively revealed his purpose to save human beings in and by his Son. This saving revelation began soon after the fall, in the garden of Eden (Gen. 3:15), and this saving revelation came to its culmination and climax in the Lord Jesus Christ (Heb. 1:1–4), who is the incarnate Word of God (John 1:1), and in whom all God's promises find their yes and amen (2 Cor. 1:20). Christ, by his death and resurrection, has saved a multitude from among every tribe, tongue, people, and nation. Jesus has not only saved people who lived after his death and resurrection. He has also saved people who lived prior to his death and resurrection. For the most part, those who were saved prior to the life and ministry of Christ were among the old covenant people of God, Israel. Even then, Israelites were saved in the same way that people today are saved—through faith in Christ. This is how Abraham (Romans 4; Galatians 3), Moses (Heb. 11:26), David (Romans 4), and Isaiah (John 12), to name just a few, were saved.

What, then, is biblical theology? Biblical theology explores the unfolding of God's self-revelation in the Bible. Biblical theology gives due weight to the central concern of biblical revelation—the glory of God in saving sinners through the work of Jesus Christ, the Son of God. It notes both the progressive and organic character of biblical revelation. Biblical revelation is *progressive* in that it moves toward a divinely predetermined goal, namely, the person and work of Jesus Christ. Biblical revelation is *organic* in that this movement resembles the growth of an organism. As a tree grows from a seed to a sapling to a mature plant, or a human being grows from a fetus to a toddler to a mature person, so also biblical revelation witnesses the maturation of God's saving promises from their shadowy beginnings to their mature completion in the Lord Jesus Christ (see Col. 2:16–17).

One of the most important ways in which God revealed his plan to redeem sinners through Christ was in making covenants with human beings. Through these covenants, God gradually revealed more and more of his one purpose and plan to save sinners in every age through Jesus Christ. In so revealing Christ to his people, God was summoning them to trust in his Son for their salvation. Covenants (and, we will see, their signs and meals) find their meaning and integration in the person and work of Christ.

Chapter 1 will offer a brief definition of *covenant*. We will then reflect on the major covenants of the Bible. Which are they? What is their relationship with each other? How does each point to the saving work of Jesus Christ?

In chapter 2, we will look at covenant signs. We will see that such signs are a staple of God's covenants with human beings. They are an important way that God condescends to us in order to reinforce his covenant promises to us. Covenant signs reach out to senses beyond the ear. We see them, feel them, smell them, and taste them. These signs help us to see how committed God is to our growth in faith.

Chapter 3 will look at covenant meals. Throughout history, God has appointed special meals for his people to enjoy. Like signs, these meals are designed to point beyond themselves. They point to the rich and abundant spiritual provision that God has stored up for us in Christ.

Chapter 4 will focus on the Lord's Supper. We will look at what the New Testament tells us about the Supper, from Jesus's institution of this meal, to the early church's faithful observance of it, to a young church's confusion and misuse of it. We will see how the apostle Paul sternly but patiently addressed the church's misapprehensions by setting the church on a sound doctrinal and practical foundation. In the Lord's Supper, we commune with the Lord Jesus Christ. Even so, Paul insists, the Supper is not a private experience. It is a family meal. We must not come to this meal and be indifferent toward our brothers and sisters in Christ. Neither is the Supper a mechanical experience. We have work to do in order to get out of that meal what Christ would have us to receive.

Chapter 5 will summarize our findings and then give some attention to some of the practical questions that have arisen around the Supper in the history and life of the church. While these questions will not set the agenda of our biblical-theological study of the Lord's

Supper, they are important nonetheless. A careful biblical-theological survey of the Supper goes a long way toward providing sound, practical answers to the very questions we bring to the Supper.

I have many goals in this little work. I hope that you will better understand the place and importance of covenant signs and covenant meals in the Bible. I hope that the Lord's Supper will take on renewed importance in your own Christian life. I hope that you will come to appreciate the way in which this and other covenant signs and covenant meals are related to the covenants God has made with his people. I hope that you will appreciate the grand unity and cohesiveness of biblical revelation, and the centrality of covenants to that unity and cohesiveness. But above all, I hope that you will trust, love, and hope in the covenant-making, covenant-keeping God who has saved sinners in Jesus Christ, and has taken them to be a people for his own possession. May your studies in the Scripture draw you closer to the God who has come near to human beings in Christ and has, in the Son of God, given undeserving sinners nothing less than himself.

1

Covenant Basics

In order to understand something, we have to know what it is. To grasp and appreciate the significance of the Lord's Supper as a covenant sign and meal, we have to understand what a covenant sign and a covenant meal are. And to understand what a covenant sign and a covenant meal are, we first have to understand what a covenant is. In this chapter, we will take up the question What is a covenant? In the next two chapters, we will take up the related questions What is a covenant sign? and What is a covenant meal?

The Word *Covenant*?

The word *covenant* is not often used in modern Western society. We sometimes hear of "covenant neighborhoods" or even "covenant marriage." For the most part, however, the term *covenant* is unfamiliar to many people.

In the Old and New Testaments, *covenant* often appears both as a term and as a concept. The term first appears in the Bible at Genesis 6:18: "But I will establish my covenant [Hebrew, *berith*] with you, and you shall come into the ark, you, your sons, your wife, and your sons' wives with you." It last appears in the Bible at Revelation 11:19: "Then God's temple in heaven was opened, and the ark of his covenant [Greek, *diathēkē*] was seen within his temple."

The term *covenant* is used in two basic settings in the Bible.[1] Sometimes covenants are made between or among human beings. One example, well known to Bible readers, is the covenant that David and Jonathan made with one another in 1 Samuel 23:18. The Bible, moreover, can speak of the marital relationship as a covenant: "The LORD was witness between you and the wife of your youth, to whom you have been faithless, though she is your companion and your wife by covenant" (Mal. 2:14). Covenants in the Bible also appear in political contexts. Sometime after the death of Saul, David entered into a covenant with "all the elders of Israel," and "they anointed David king over Israel" (2 Sam. 5:3).

The most important covenants in the Bible, however, are the covenants that God made with human beings. I have already mentioned the covenant that God made with Noah (Gen. 6:18). Afterward, God entered into a covenant with Abraham (Gen. 12:1–3; 15:1–21; 17:1–14). Over four hundred years later, God entered into a covenant with Abraham's descendants (Israel) at Mount Sinai (Ex. 19:1–6). God subsequently made a covenant with David, in which God pledged to "establish the throne of [David's] kingdom forever" (2 Sam. 7:13). The prophet Jeremiah later spoke of a "new covenant" in which God pledged to "forgive" his people's "iniquity" and "remember their sin no more" (Jer. 31:34). The New Testament writers tell us that this new covenant came to fulfillment in the person and work of Jesus Christ (see Luke 22:20; 1 Cor. 11:25).

---

1. See John Murray, *The Covenant of Grace: A Biblico-Theological Study* (Phillipsburg, NJ: Presbyterian and Reformed, 1988), 8–12; and Paul R. Williamson, *Sealed with an Oath: Covenant in God's Unfolding Purpose*, New Studies in Biblical Theology 23 (Downers Grove, IL: InterVarsity Press, 2007), 38–43.

What Is a Covenant?

Covenants, then, course like a river through redemptive history and biblical revelation.[2] Their importance to the Bible underscores the question What is a covenant? To answer that question, we may draw three observations. These three observations yield a working definition of the covenants that God made with human beings. Once we have that working definition in place, we will be able to think about how these covenants structure both the history of God's dealings with humanity and the divinely authored record of that history, the Bible.

First, "covenant" assumes an "existing, elective relationship" between two parties and serves as the "solemn ratification" of that relationship.[3] Covenants in the Bible do not create a relationship that did not exist before. They formalize a relationship that is already in place. When God, for example, made a covenant with Abraham, he did so in the context of an existing relationship with Abraham. God had called Abraham to leave Ur of the Chaldees (Genesis 11) before he entered into covenant with him (Genesis 12). Similarly, God was already in relationship with Israel when he entered into covenant with them at Mount Sinai. In each case, God's covenant provided depth and structure to a relationship that was already in place.

These relationships, furthermore, are elective. God was not obliged to enter into relationship with either Abraham or Israel. It was God's sovereign and unmerited choice to establish a relationship with the persons with whom he would enter into covenant (see Deut. 7:6–7). God's covenants with human beings are never a "given," nor are the relationships that lie back of those covenants.

---

2. For further discussion of the covenants in the Bible, see Thomas Schreiner, *Covenant and God's Purpose for the World*, Short Studies in Biblical Theology (Wheaton, IL: Crossway, 2017).

3. Williamson, *Sealed with an Oath*, 43.

Second, a covenant involves life-and-death issues.[4] Part of the solemnity of a covenant is that it does not traffic in the trivial details of life. Covenants address the most important concerns of human existence. We will see below that God made a covenant with Adam in the garden (Gen. 2:15–17). God held before Adam nothing less than eternal death and eternal life: "but of the tree of the knowledge of good and evil you shall not eat, for in the day that you eat of it you shall surely die" (Gen. 2:17). The death to which Adam and his ordinary descendants are subjected through sin is not only physical or biological death. It is also eternal death (Matt. 25:46).

One of the primary blessings that Abraham enjoyed in covenant with God was justification by faith alone (see Gal. 3:6–9). In his letters, Paul explains that justification is God's declaration that the sinner is righteous. This declaration is based solely upon the obedience and death of Jesus Christ, imputed to the sinner, and received through faith alone (see Rom. 3:21–26; 4:1–8; 5:12–21). In Christ, the justified sinner has passed from condemnation to vindication. For the person who is justified, the day of judgment will not be a day of divine wrath and the beginning of eternal punishment. It will be for him or her a day of blessing and glory. This divine promise of justification was administered to Abraham and to all his believing offspring in God's gracious covenant with them in Jesus Christ.

Similarly, the Mosaic covenant set before Israel matters of life and death. Moses, the human mediator of the covenant between God and Israel, ratified the covenant by sprinkling the altar and the people with sacrificial blood (see Ex. 24:1–8). While the Mosaic covenant concerned itself with Israel's experience in the Land of Promise, its concerns were not exclusively this-worldly. The Mosaic covenant was no less occupied with eternal concerns. The exchange between

---

4. The phrase "life and death" is that of O. Palmer Robertson, *The Christ of the Covenants* (Phillipsburg, NJ: Presbyterian and Reformed, 1980), 4, 10.

Jesus and the rich young ruler, for instance, shows us that the Mosaic covenant pointed the way to "eternal life" (see Matt. 19:16–22).[5] Jesus, in dying on the cross, "redeemed us from the curse of the law by becoming a curse for us—for it is written, 'Cursed is everyone who is hanged on a tree'" (Gal. 3:13, citing Deut. 21:23). Jesus's death, which rescues us from eternal condemnation and wrath (1 Thess. 1:10; 5:9), has redeemed us from that curse to which the laws of the Mosaic covenant testified.

Third, a covenant is a sovereign administration of promises with corresponding obligations.[6] God's covenants are sovereign administrations. That is to say, God comes to human beings and imposes his covenants upon them. We have already observed this characteristic of God's covenants in the cases of Abraham, Israel, and David. In the Bible we never see human beings coming to God and proposing a covenant with him. Recall further that God's covenants are made in the context of elective relationships. God sovereignly chooses to enter into a relationship with someone before he enters into covenant with that party. There is yet another sense in which we may appreciate God's covenants as sovereign administrations. It is God and God alone who sets the terms of his covenants with people. People never negotiate or haggle with God over these terms. God, in his kindness and goodness, sets these terms and imposes them upon human beings.

Older writers often spoke of God's covenants with humans as *agreements* between God and people.[7] This term can be misleading

---

5. The rich young ruler mistakenly believed that he could keep the commandments of the Mosaic covenant and so merit eternal life. Jesus's goal in this exchange was to help this man see that it is impossible for sinful human beings to attain this goal. Only when one realizes his own inability to merit life by the law's commandments will he appreciate the need for the Savior whose life and death meet all the demands of God's law on sinners' behalf.

6. The phrase "sovereign administration" is indebted to Robertson, *Christ of the Covenants*, 4, et passim.

7. As for, example, Henry Bullinger, Zacharias Ursinus, John Preston, William Perkins, Peter van Mastricht, Francis Turretin, and Herman Witsius, as cited at Murray, *Covenant of Grace*, 5–7.

insofar as it may suggest that God and humans enter into covenants as equal partners. Properly understood, however, *agreement* captures an important dimension of God's covenants with people. When God enters into covenant with someone, God calls that person to embrace that covenant unreservedly. God's covenant partners should sincerely and willingly walk with him in covenant (Gen. 17:1). The fact that God sovereignly imposes his covenant on human beings does not destroy our humanity. On the contrary, it engages and exalts our humanity. God's covenants give us the privilege of entering into fellowship and communion with the God who made and redeemed us.

If God's covenants with humans are sovereign administrations, then what do they administer? They administer promises with corresponding obligations. God's promises sit at the heart of his covenants with human beings. Implicit in the covenant that God made with Adam in the garden of Eden was the promise of life.[8] Had Adam obeyed God, he would have entered into confirmed, eternal life. In his covenant with Noah, God promised to preserve the world from another global deluge. In his covenant with Abraham, God pledged to Abraham offspring and land (see Gen. 26:3–4). In his covenant with Israel at Sinai, God offered Israel life and blessing in the land that he provided them and to which he brought them from their former bondage in Egypt. In his covenant with David, God promised that David's "house" and "kingdom shall be made sure forever before me" (2 Sam. 7:16).

It is important to observe that God did not condition the giving of these promises upon the worth or merit of his covenant partner. In other words, God did not make these promises because he saw

---

8. Later in this chapter, we will see that obedience played a different role in God's covenant with Adam in the garden of Eden than it does for God's people in other covenants. Even so, Adam was to obey God in light of a divine promise.

or could foresee that their recipients did or would deserve them. He made them unconditionally, that is, without regard to our character or performance. Paul insists in Romans 4 that Abraham received the promises through faith and not by works "in order that the promise may rest on grace and be guaranteed to all his offspring" (4:16). Even faith contributes nothing to the promise. Faith trusts the One who makes the promise and receives with open and empty hands what the promise-making God graciously provides the undeserving.

To say that God's covenant promises are sovereignly and freely bestowed, apart from the merits of the recipient, is not to say that God's human covenant partners are rendered passive, much less free to live in sin. On the contrary, God's covenants fully engage us to think and live in a way that is pleasing to him. We are to receive God's promises through faith, which is the gift of God (Phil. 1:29; cf. Eph. 2:8–10). With those promises, God also gives us commands. Faith necessarily takes up those commands in thankful obedience to God.

Consider the Mosaic legislation that God gave Israel to order life in the land that he had given his people. But the Mosaic covenant is no anomaly. God called Abraham, already in covenant with him, to "walk before [him], and be blameless" (Gen. 17:1). "Walk" is a way of describing in Scripture the totality of life before God—not only our behavior but also our thinking, our attitudes, and our affections.[9] The call to "be blameless" does not mean that Abraham needed to achieve sinless perfection or else forfeit his covenant standing with God. "Blamelessness" is a term that describes persons in Scripture who were far from sinless.[10] It refers rather to God's expectation that his people will serve him wholeheartedly and sincerely. God does not want covenant partners who are duplicitous or wavering in their

---

9. Notice the way in which Paul structures the commands of Ephesians 4–6 by the imperative "walk." Walking captures the whole sum of Christian duty.

10. Noah (Gen. 6:9), Job (Job 1:1), and Zechariah and Elizabeth (Luke 1:6), to take four examples.

allegiance to him. He wants covenant partners who unreservedly dedicate their whole selves to God and his service. In Genesis 18:19, God shows us what blamelessness looks like. God charges Abraham to "command his children and his household after him to keep the way of the LORD by doing righteousness and justice." "Righteousness and justice," as defined by God's Word, were to characterize the way in which covenant members (Abraham, his children, his household) were to live before God.

Commands are not restricted to God's covenants with Israel and Abraham. The Davidic covenant, in which God brought David and his offspring into relation to himself as "son[s]," expected devoted covenantal behavior from these sons (2 Sam. 7:14–15; 1 Kings 2:1–4). The new covenant, according to Jeremiah, expects of God's people an obedience to the law that originates from the heart (Jer. 31:33). It is to this obedience that Jesus testified powerfully and early in his ministry in the Sermon on the Mount (Matt. 5:17–7:29).

In summary, then, with promises come obligations in God's covenants with humans. These obligations are chiefly faith, obedience, and, after the fall, repentance. In repentance, one turns from sin to God. In faith, one receives the promises. In obedience, one takes up all the commands that God has given to that person.

COVENANT PROMISES AND OBLIGATIONS

To say that God's covenants with human beings administer both promises and obligations raises the question of how promise and obligation relate to one another. Let us take up this question in reference to the covenants that come after the fall of humanity into sin. We have already seen that God's promises are not conditioned on the creature's worthiness. God does not wait for us to reach a threshold of merit or goodness before he willingly makes promises to us. The

Scripture's account of the lives of Abraham and David amply illustrate that point.

At the same time, we have no right to claim the covenant promises of God while refusing to take up the covenant obligations, particularly the commandments, that God gives us. To a nation that thought the presence of the temple rendered it immune to the demands of God's law, God spoke through the prophet Jeremiah, "Amend your ways and your deeds, and I will let you dwell in this place. Do not trust in these deceptive words: 'This is the temple of the LORD, the temple of the LORD, the temple of the LORD'" (Jer. 7:3–4). As James teaches in the New Testament, any so-called faith that lays claim to God's saving promises but lacks the fruit of good works is "dead" and "useless" (James 2:17, 20, 26). True faith, Paul tells us, works by love (Gal. 5:6).

Our obedience is necessary to walking in covenant with God, but it does not bring us into covenant relationship with God. Neither does it merit the promises that God freely and sovereignly makes to us. Obedience, rather, is the way in which God's covenant partners respond to his covenant promises. There is, therefore, a necessary and invariable priority of promise to the obligation of obedience. This priority is vividly illustrated in the opening lines of Exodus 20. Before God gives the "Ten Words" of Exodus 20:3–17, he tells his people, "I am the LORD your God, who brought you out of the land of Egypt, out of the house of slavery" (20:2). Israel's obedience is to be a faith-filled response to the grace of God in redeeming them from bondage in Egypt. This principle abides across God's covenants with human beings in redemptive history. The commands that God gives us in covenant with him are the God-appointed way in which we must respond to the covenant promises he has freely given us.

How, then, are we to understand statements that appear to say that God suspends his promises upon our obedience in covenant with him? For example:

> I am God Almighty; walk before me, and be blameless, *that I may make my covenant between me and you, and may multiply you greatly.* (Gen. 17:1–2)

> For I have chosen [Abraham], that he may command his children and his household after him to keep the way of the LORD by doing righteousness and justice, *so that the LORD may bring to Abraham what he has promised him.* (Gen. 18:19)

> Now therefore, *if you will indeed obey my voice and keep my covenant,* you shall be my treasured possession among all peoples, for all the earth is mine; and you shall be to me a kingdom of priests and a holy nation. (Ex. 19:5–6)

When God speaks to Abraham as he does in Genesis 17 and Genesis 18, God has already entered into covenant with him and made promises unconditioned upon Abraham's character or performance (Genesis 12; 15). When God speaks to Israel as he does in Exodus 19, God has already set apart Israel to himself (Ex. 2:24–25) and redeemed his people from Egypt (see Ex. 19:4).[11] God cannot mean that Abraham's and Israel's obedience is a procuring precondition for God's promises. He speaks these words in Genesis 17–18 and Exodus 19 to people to whom he has already freely and graciously given his promises.

In the verses cited above, God is giving Abraham and Israel the same message. If God's covenant partners are to enter into and to enjoy the covenant promises that he has freely made to them, then

---

11. Moses tells us that the Israelites, on the cusp of deliverance, demonstrated their moral unworthiness as the object of God's redemption (see Ex. 14:10–14).

they must take up the covenant obligations that he has laid upon them. Covenant obligations in no way *merit or earn* God's covenant promises, but they are the way in which God has appointed us to *experience and enjoy* the blessings that he freely gives us in his promises. If we do not experience and enjoy the promises by this appointed path, then we have no legitimate claim to the promises at all. But if we do so experience and enjoy these unconditional promises, that reality is due ultimately to the sovereign grace of God.

In the case of Abraham, the Patriarch's obedience would be the way that God appointed to bring to pass what God sovereignly promised him. The promised offspring was the sovereign provision of God, in no way owing to Abraham's or Sarah's reproductive powers (see Gen. 17:17; 18:12). Abraham's body was "as good as dead," and Sarah's womb was barren (Rom. 4:19). But God provided that offspring through Sarah's conception and birth (Gen. 21:2). That act of conception, Paul tells us, was the fruit of Abraham's faith in God's promise (Rom. 4:20–21). The way in which Abraham would experience the promise that God had freely made to him (an offspring) was by trusting and yielding obedience to God.

THE PROVISION OF OBEDIENCE

Before we leave the subject of obedience in God's covenants, it is important to correct a common misunderstanding. Obedience is not the unaided response of the covenant partner to the goodness of God in his covenants with us. Our obedience, rather, is itself the provision of God in his covenants with us. God not only tells us what he expects us to do in his covenants with us; he also makes available and freely supplies the ability to do what he commands.

We may look briefly at two examples of this provision in the Old Testament. First, in Leviticus 11:45, God commands his people to be holy in light of his own divine character and in light of the redemption of his people from bondage in Egypt: "For I am the LORD who brought you up out of the land of Egypt to be your God. You shall therefore be holy, for I am holy." A few chapters later, God identifies himself as "the LORD who sanctifies you" (Lev. 20:8; 22:32). In other words, God commits himself to making Israel holy. He not only gives commands to his people but also supplies them with the ability to do those commands.

Second, in Jeremiah 31, God announces his great new covenant promise to a people who are on the cusp of ruin. The Babylonian armies have hemmed in Jerusalem and are poised to sack the city and carry the population into exile. This devastation, God tells Judah through his prophets, will be God's judgment upon a people who have disobeyed God, broken covenant with him, and drawn down the curses of the covenant upon themselves. But neither disobedience nor judgment is God's last word to his people. God will make a "new covenant" with them (31:31).

In this new covenant, God says, "I will put my law within them, and I will write it on their hearts" (31:33). God's inscribing the law on the hearts of his people is not altogether new. Believers in every age have testified to it (see Ps. 40:8). What, then, makes this promise "new"? Its newness is the sheer scope and breadth of this work. Under the old covenant, the inscription of the law upon the heart does not appear to have been the experience of the generality of Israel and Judah. After all, God through his prophets repeatedly indicted the nation for covenant treachery. Under the new covenant, however, God pledges that this work will pervade the covenant community in unprecedented fashion, even as the borders of the covenant community will extend to the end of the earth (cf. Matt. 28:20; Acts 1:8). The experience of Israel testified to the people's inability to yield of themselves what God had required in the Mosaic covenant and their refusal to avail themselves of the grace that God had made available to them for the keeping of his covenant. Under the new covenant,

God graciously pledges to provide in abundant supply the ability to observe his commandments from the heart.[12] Obedience is the requirement and the provision of God's covenant.

We may summarize our findings thus far about God's covenants with people in the Bible as follows: *God's covenants with people formalize an existing, elective relationship and in this way bring life-and-death issues to the fore. In these covenants, God sovereignly administers promises with corresponding obligations.*

The First Covenant with Adam

In building a definition of the covenants that God makes with people, we have seen such covenants running through the whole of the Bible, from Genesis to Revelation. Those covenants include the Noahic (Genesis 6; 9); Abrahamic (Genesis 12; 15; 17); Mosaic (Exodus 19–20); Davidic (2 Samuel 7); and new (Jeremiah 31) covenants. Before we give some thought to how these covenants are related to one another, we must first consider an important and foundational covenant that God makes at the very dawn of history with the first human being, Adam, and, in Adam, with Adam's ordinary descendants. We learn of this covenant in Genesis 2. God comes to Adam and gives him a special command, "You may surely eat of every tree of the garden, but of the tree of the knowledge of good and evil you shall not eat, for in the day that you eat of it you shall surely die" (2:16–17). Even though Eve violates this command before Adam does, Adam has a particular, even unique, accountability to God for transgressing the command. It is to

---

12. Compare the teaching of Moses in Deuteronomy. In Deut. 10:16, Moses commands Israel to "circumcise therefore the foreskin of your heart, and be no longer stubborn." Events would prove Israel's failure to observe that commandment. In the great prophecy of Deut. 30:1–10, Moses tells the people that, after their disobedience and exile, they will return to the land for blessing. At this time, "the LORD your God will circumcise your heart and the heart of your offspring, so that you will love the LORD your God with all your heart and with all your soul, that you may live" (30:6). God, in other words, pledges to do what Israel was commanded to do but, in fact, failed to do.

Adam that God announces his curse upon the earth and the sentence of death upon humanity for this sin (Gen. 3:17–19).

The command itself comes with the threatened curse "for in the day that you eat of it you shall surely die." But what if Adam had obeyed? We may properly infer that had Adam obeyed the command not to eat of that tree, he not only would have escaped death but also would have enjoyed life. But how could Adam, already very much alive, have looked forward to life? The life offered to Adam upon condition of obedience would have been *secure* life—life that he could not lose or forfeit. Further, the life held out to Adam would have been *heightened* or *intensified* life. In other words, Adam would have enjoyed higher and greater degrees of the communion and fellowship with God that he was already enjoying in the garden.

Even though the word *covenant* does not appear in Genesis 2–3, we have the essence of a covenant in the garden. By the time we arrive at the end of Genesis 2, we have learned that God and Adam are in an *existing and elective relationship*. Not only does God relate to Adam as the creature he has made (Gen. 1:26–27), but God also chooses Adam to undertake a project that will profoundly affect his descendants. The arrangement that God imposes upon Adam, furthermore, is one of *life-and-death issues*. The tragic outcome is death in all its fullness—physical and eternal. Had Adam obeyed God, consummate, eternal life would have been the outcome. This arrangement, moreover, has God imposing an *obligation*, one that necessarily implies a *promise* of confirmed life upon obedience to God's command. This arrangement, furthermore, is *sovereignly administered*. God imposes these terms upon Adam. Adam receives them but sadly rejects them when he disobeys God's command. Death for him and his ordinary posterity is the consequence.

Other passages of Scripture confirm that this arrangement in the garden was a covenant. While the translation has been debated, a strong case may be made for the ESV rendering of Hosea 6:7: "But like Adam they transgressed the covenant; there they dealt faithlessly with me." On this reading, Hosea is saying that Adam's sin in Genesis 3 was a violation of the covenant that God had previously made with him. God had entered into covenant with Adam before sin entered into the world.

The testimony of the apostle Paul is no less compelling. In Romans 5:12–21, the apostle sets Adam and Christ in parallel (cf. 1 Cor. 15:20–22, 44–49). Each is a representative man whose actions have affected the eternal destinies of those whom he represents. Adam's one sin resulted in condemnation and death for all those whom he represents. Jesus's obedience and death resulted in justification and life for all those whom he represents. Elsewhere, Paul speaks of Jesus's death for our justification in expressly covenantal terms (see 1 Cor. 11:25–26; 2 Cor. 3:7–11). If Paul understands *Jesus's* representative work in covenantal terms, and if Paul understands *Jesus* and *Adam* to be parallel as representative persons, then we are bound to understand *Adam's* representative work in covenantal terms. Paul would have us to understand that both the command that God gave to Adam and Adam's disobedience to that command took place entirely in a covenantal framework. Adam was in covenant with God in the garden.

Needed—A Different Kind of Covenant

While Paul says that Adam and Jesus are parallel to one another, he does not say that Adam and believers are parallel to one another. This fact helps us to see that Adam was in a different kind of covenant with God than believers are. Appreciating the difference between these two covenants is crucial to understanding the Bible's teaching about God's covenants with human beings.

The covenant that God made with Adam depended on Adam's performance. If he had obeyed God's commandment not to eat the forbidden fruit (and had continued in obedience to all the other commands that God had given him), then he would have earned life for himself and for his posterity. Life was the reward that God held out for obedience. But Adam transgressed that command. As a result, he brought death upon himself and his posterity. Death was the penalty that God imposed for disobedience. For this reason, students of the Bible have often referred to this covenant as the "covenant of works." That name helps us to see that the covenant hung on the performance of our representative, Adam.

But we have seen above that our obedience does not work in the same way in our own covenant relationship with God. The blessings of the covenant are the free and unmerited gifts of God to us. We may and ought to obey God, but our obedience does not secure those blessings in the way that Adam's obedience would have secured the blessing of life. Obedience is, rather, the way in which we come to experience and enjoy the blessings that God freely gives us in covenant with him. Since all that we have in covenant with God is the provision of his grace, students of the Bible have often referred to this covenant as the "covenant of grace."

The blessings of the covenant are not something that we earn, but that is not to say that they are unearned. Jesus Christ, our Mediator and covenant Head, has earned them for us. He has merited all the blessings of salvation for us by his perfect obedience, his death on the cross, and his resurrection from the dead. It has been put this way: the covenant of grace is a covenant of *grace* to *us* because it was first a covenant of *works* to *Jesus*. Jesus Christ undid all that Adam did, and Jesus Christ did all that Adam failed to do. Our life in covenant with God is absolutely assured because of the work of our God and Savior, our covenant Head, Jesus Christ.

Jesus Christ is *the* covenant keeper, our faithful and accomplished Mediator and Head. There is no question that the new covenant of which Jeremiah, Jesus, and Paul spoke is intimately bound up in the obedience, death, and resurrection of Jesus Christ. Believers today are in covenant with God in and through the Lord Jesus.

What Ties the Covenants Together?

We have seen that God made many covenants with sinful humans across history that preceded the new covenant. Let us look now at what unites those covenants, and think about their relation to Jesus. The New Testament understands all of God's several covenants with sinners in the Old Testament to point toward and find their intended consummation in the person and work of Jesus Christ. Two examples help us see this point.

First, in Luke 1, Zechariah, the father of John the Baptist, praises God for the birth of his son, who will prepare the way of the Lord Jesus Christ (see Luke 1:76). In this song, Zechariah testifies to his understanding of the significance of the appearance of Jesus. What Jesus has come to do is to fulfill the Abrahamic covenant. In sending Christ to save sinners, God has "remember[ed] his holy covenant, the oath that he swore to our father Abraham" (Luke 1:72–73). Furthermore, the arrival of Jesus is in fulfillment of the promises that God made to David; "[God] has raised up a horn of salvation for us in the house of his servant David" (Luke 1:69). Zechariah tells us that there is a direct line connecting the Abrahamic covenant, the Davidic covenant, and the person and work of Christ. He also helps us to see the character of that line. The common concern of the Abrahamic and Davidic covenants is the salvation that Jesus Christ has accomplished in history in his death and resurrection.

Second, in looking back on Israel's history, the apostle Paul speaks of the "covenants" (Rom. 9:4) or the "covenants of promise" (Eph. 2:12) that God gave to Israel. This broad designation suggests that Paul understood the various covenants of Israel's history in terms of a grand and sweeping unity. Paul elsewhere tells us that the Abrahamic and the Mosaic covenants found their intended goal in the person and work of Christ (see Gal. 3:1–4:7). Here in Romans 9:4–5 and Ephesians 2:11–16 he tells us that *all* the covenants of Israel's history found their goal in Christ. We should see all the covenants that God made with humans after the fall in a divinely arranged succession leading to their goal, Jesus Christ.

How far back into redemptive history may we take this succession of covenants that find their goal and consummation in Jesus Christ? Paul understood the first gospel promise in history to find its fulfillment in the work of Christ.

> I will put enmity between you and the woman,
>> and between your offspring and her offspring;
> he shall bruise your head,
>> and you shall bruise his heel. (Gen. 3:15)

> The God of peace will soon crush Satan under your feet. The grace of our Lord Jesus Christ be with you. (Rom. 16:20)

In Genesis 3:15, God tells the serpent (that is, Satan, Rev. 12:9) that he will raise up a human descendant from Eve who will deal Satan a mortal blow ("he shall bruise your head"). In Romans 16:20, Paul echoes that promise for the encouragement of believers. Satan, who was despoiled and dethroned at the cross (Col. 2:15), will be dealt the final blow at the return of Christ. (That Satan will be crushed under the feet of believers reflects the union between Christ and his people—we will share in Christ's final victory over Satan at Christ's return.)

We may speak of this first gospel promise in covenantal terms for at least two reasons. First, Paul tells us here in Romans 16:20 that this promise for Adam found its fulfillment in the death and resurrection of Jesus Christ. If the fulfillment took place in the context of God's gracious covenant, then we should consider whether the promise was administered in the context of God's gracious covenant as well. Second, God's promise for Adam concerned an offspring, just as God's promises to Abraham and to David concerned an offspring. Since the Abrahamic and Davidic promises are explicitly covenantal, then we should think of the earlier and similar Adamic promise as covenantal also.

Further, Genesis gives us indications that this promise was administered to Adam and Eve by way of covenant. Recall the basic elements of a covenant. We have an *existing, elective relationship.* Adam and Eve are already in relationship with God as creatures. That relationship has been radically transformed by the fall. Adam and Eve flee from God, hide from God, and try to cover themselves from God. But God pursues them, not to destroy them but to have mercy upon them. He has chosen them in love to be recipients of his saving grace. It is in the context of that electing love that God speaks to Adam and Eve in Genesis 3.

God's promise, furthermore, *brings life-and-death issues to the fore.* When God speaks in Genesis 3, Adam and Eve are sinners, justly subject to God's judgment, and deserving of death (Gen. 2:17). The word of promise concerns a mortal blow to Satan ("he shall bruise your head") and a serious blow to the promised offspring of Eve ("you shall bruise his heel"). This promise, of course, points to the reality of Satan's defeat through the death of Christ on the cross, a death that would not have permanent hold on his humanity. It is in light of this promised death of Eve's offspring that God approaches Adam and Eve in mercy and life, not judgment and death.

God's word implies for Adam *a promise with corresponding obligations.* The promise, we have seen, is one of salvation through the work of the offspring of Eve, the Lord Jesus Christ. Adam and Eve are to respond in faith to the promise. They are to believe God's word.

Their faith in this promise will come to expression in their efforts to conceive and raise their children (see Gen. 3:16). Further, Adam, although exiled from Eden, has work to do. He must cultivate the now cursed earth (see Gen. 3:17–19, 23–24).

Even though Genesis 3 does not use the word *covenant* to describe God's dealings with Adam and Eve, we may fairly represent those dealings as covenantal. They have the basic elements of a covenant. The promise of an offspring in Genesis 3 is developed later in redemptive history in explicitly covenantal terms (Genesis 12; 15; 17; 2 Samuel 7). Paul's teaching in Romans 16 explicitly understands the offspring promise of Genesis 3 to find its fulfillment in the person and work of Christ, whose work is covenantal. Paul's argument in Romans 5:12–21 tells us that, since the fall, God has saved sinners only through the work of his Son Jesus Christ, who is the second Adam, the covenantal representative of his people in every age. We may conclude, then, that the succession of covenants through which God saves sinners in Christ goes back to the very dawn of redemptive history.

The Relationship between the Covenants

The whole of redemptive history, from Genesis 3:15 to the present, is covenantal in character. Let us look more closely at the succession of covenants presented to us in Scripture and the relation that they have to each other.

We have already seen that the saving, finished work of Christ, administered under the new covenant, is the intended fulfillment of the Old Testament covenants that have preceded it. The new covenant, then, is the final and climactic installment of the single and unified gracious covenant inaugurated in the garden after the fall.

The New Testament writers give particular attention to three covenants within the succession of covenants in the Old Testament. The first is the Abrahamic covenant, which we have already observed in the writings of Luke and Paul. In this covenant, God promised to raise up from Abraham an offspring who would bring blessing to the nations. This offspring, of course, is the Lord Jesus Christ. The second is the Mosaic covenant, which the apostle John represents as anticipating the work of Christ (see John 1:17; 5:46), and the apostle Paul represents as preparing Israel for the coming of Christ (Gal. 3:15–4:7). The third is the Davidic covenant, which in many ways was an extension and specification of the Abrahamic covenant.[13] From the multitude of Abraham's seed, God would raise up one offspring from the line of David who would be God's own Son and would reign over God's people.

What about the covenant that God made with Noah? While the New Testament writers mention Noah in many places, they do not give sustained attention to the covenant that God made with him. This does not mean that the Noahic covenant is unimportant. One biblical theologian has aptly termed it the "covenant of preservation."[14] In the Noahic covenant, God promised that "the waters shall never again become a flood to destroy all flesh" (Gen. 9:15). The commands that God gave to Noah and his descendants in Genesis 9:1–7 were for the multiplication of human beings and the preservation of their lives. In these ways, God ensured that there would be a humanity to redeem. God's covenant with Noah provided the context in which his redemptive purposes would advance in human history.

God's redemptive purposes are evident in another way in the Noahic covenant. God made this covenant with Noah, a man who was the special object of God's gracious favor (Gen. 6:8). That is to say, Noah was set apart from the rest of humanity by the grace of God. He

---

13. The Davidic covenant is recorded in 2 Samuel 7 and 1 Chronicles 17. Interestingly, neither of those passages terms God's dealings with David as a covenant. Subsequent revelation, however, makes clear that these dealings were, in fact, a covenant (Pss. 89:3; 132:11–12; Jer. 33:21). We may see, then, that Scripture may document a covenant even when the word *covenant* does not appear in the record of the transaction itself.

14. Robertson, *Christ of the Covenants*, 109.

therefore did not experience the judgment that befell the rest of humanity. Noah and his family, rather, were spared the judgment through the ark that God commanded him to build. This deliverance of Noah and his family is a picture, Peter tells us, of believers' salvation in Jesus Christ (1 Pet. 3:21–22). Like Noah, we have been delivered from the judgment that we deserve for our sins by the mercies of God in Christ. For this reason, the Noahic covenant not only provided the context in which God's redemptive purposes would unfold, but also was an administration of grace and mercy to undeserving sinners.

Conclusion

We have seen that the covenants that God makes with human beings not only run through both the Old and the New Testaments but also stand in a close and integrated relationship with one another. Two covenants encompass the whole scope of biblical revelation—the covenant of works and the covenant of grace. God made the covenant of works with Adam in the garden, before the fall. In that covenant, Adam was a representative man. God commanded Adam not to eat of the fruit of the tree of knowledge of good and evil upon the pain of death. God implicitly promised Adam confirmed, consummate life upon obedience. When Adam sinned against God, that sin was covenantally counted to his ordinary descendants. Adam's race is therefore conceived and born in sin, guilty, condemned, and under the wrath of God.

But God made the covenant of grace with Christ as the second Adam. Like Adam, Christ is a representative man. Unlike Adam, Christ obeyed God, even unto death. As a result, Christ obeyed where Adam (and we in Adam) failed to obey. And, in obedience to God, Christ died on the cross to pay the penalty for our sin.

Although Christ did not accomplish this redemptive work right away, his work is the basis on which God's people in every age have been saved. God has always saved sinners through faith in Christ. For that reason, God announced to fallen Adam and Eve his intention to defeat sin, Satan, and death by the work of his Son, calling Adam and Eve to believe this promise and to respond in the obedience of faith. Throughout redemptive history, God disclosed more and more of his eternal purpose to save sinners by the work of his Son. He did this through his covenants. In distinct but complementary ways, God's covenants with Noah, Abraham, Moses, and David revealed more and more of Christ to God's people, and in this way prepared them for Christ's arrival in the fullness of time. These covenants were all administrations or epochs of the one unfolding covenant of grace.

It is fair, then, to characterize biblical theology as *covenant* theology. There are, of course, other motifs and themes that run the gamut of Scripture and serve as organizing principles of biblical revelation. Covenant theology, however, uniquely integrates biblical revelation. Covenant theology's center is the redemptive work of Christ, accomplished in history and applied to God's people in every age. In a powerful way, covenant theology shows us how our Christian lives relate to Christ's work on our behalf. Covenant theology, then, helps us to be better readers of the Bible, to see Christ with greater clarity, and to learn how to live for Christ in this age.[15]

Having surveyed the Bible's teaching about covenants, we are now ready to consider those tangible covenant signs that God has appointed to accompany these covenants. Let us now look at what Scripture has to say about these covenant signs.

---

15. Students of the Bible have observed that the Bible testifies to an eternal covenant among the persons of the Godhead. This covenant is sometimes called the covenant of redemption, and finds testimony in John's Gospel (see especially John 6, 10, 17). In this covenant, the Father agreed in eternity to send his Son into the world to obey, die, and rise again for the elect. The Son agreed to take on our humanity, come into this world as one sent by the Father, and obey the Father completely. The Son's reward for his obedience was the glory that the Father bestowed upon him at his exaltation. The Spirit consented to dwell upon Christ's humanity during his public ministry and to raise his body gloriously from the dead. Since this book concerns the signs and meals that attend God's covenants in history, I will not give further attention to the covenant of redemption. The importance of the covenant of redemption, however, is that it helps believers better appreciate the eternal foundations on which our salvation rests.

2

Covenant Signs

One of the main purposes of God's covenants in redemptive history is to administer the promises of God to his people. The way in which we are to respond to those promises is faith—we understand, accept, and embrace the promises that God makes to us on the credit of his own character. The whole of our lives in covenant with God is lived out of this faith (see Gal. 2:20).

God's people have always been tempted to unbelief. This temptation is especially strong when circumstances appear to contradict what God has promised us. The life of Abraham gives some vivid examples of this temptation. After God told Abraham to go from Ur of the Chaldeans "to the land that I will show you," a "severe . . . famine" struck the Land of Promise, and Abraham temporarily left the land (Gen. 12:1, 10). Many years after God promised to provide Abraham and Sarah a child, they were still childless. Abraham told God, "You have given me no offspring," and he wondered whether "a member of [his own] household" would be his heir (Gen. 15:3). Later, at the prompting of his wife, Abraham resorted to the device of conceiving a child by his servant, Hagar, in the hope that this child, Ishmael, would be the heir of whom God had spoken (Gen. 16:1–4). This scheme, however, was an act of unbelief and not of faith. Isaac, later conceived in Sarah's own womb, was to be the appointed heir, not Ishmael.

Even so, readers of Scripture know Abraham as "the man of faith" (Gal. 3:9; lit. "believing Abraham"). Paul insists that Abraham's faith grew stronger in time, not weaker (Rom. 4:20–21). That Abraham's faith waxed and did not wane in the face of sustained temptations to unbelief raises the question Why?

The ultimate answer to that question was the grace of God. It was God's grace that created, sustained, and strengthened Abraham's faith in the face of temptations to unbelief. It recovered him from his lapses into unbelief. But God did not grow Abraham's faith apart from means. God used means to strengthen and increase the Patriarch's faith.

An Encouraging Sign

One of those means was a covenant sign that God appointed for Abraham. That sign was circumcision. God instituted circumcision as recorded in Genesis 17 to help Abraham's faith. The sign of circumcision was a perpetual reminder in Abraham's own flesh of the covenant promises of God. When the circumstances visible to Abraham tempted him to unbelief, there was an equally visible sign from God to strengthen his faith and encourage him in trusting obedience to God.

This sign was not something that God gave for a brief season of Abraham's life. On the contrary, circumcision left an indelible mark in Abraham's flesh. He knew he bore the sign wherever he went and for the duration of his life. Nor was this sign unique to Abraham. God appointed circumcision for Abraham's household.

He who is eight days old among you shall be circumcised. Every male throughout your generations, whether born in your house or bought with your money from any foreigner who is not of your offspring, both he who is born in your house and he who is bought with your money, shall surely be circumcised. So shall my covenant be in your flesh an everlasting covenant. (Gen. 17:12–13)

Every male member of Abraham's household—whether those who were born into it or those who entered into it as servants—was to receive the covenant sign. This ordinance was to stand perpetually— "throughout their generations" (Gen. 17:9).

Furthermore, God threatened judgment for those who did not receive the sign: "Any uncircumcised male who is not circumcised in the flesh of his foreskin shall be cut off from his people; he has broken my covenant" (Gen. 17:14). God was concerned that each male of the covenant household receive the covenant sign. Those males who did not receive the "cutting off" of their foreskin would themselves be "cut off" from God's people. Failure to receive the sign subjected one to covenant curse and judgment. Bearing the covenant sign (or not) was not a matter of indifference to God. When we think below about the specific meaning of circumcision, we will see more clearly why this was the case.

When we look at the various covenants that God made with people in Scripture, a striking pattern emerges—God appointed a sign to accompany the covenant that he made. The covenant signs were physical and tangible objects susceptible to the five senses. They were not newly created but already existing in the world of the first recipients. Each sign was given to the covenant community as a visible and perpetual reminder of God's goodness in and through that particular covenant. God also intended his signs to confirm the truth of his covenant promises to the faith of his people.

Various Covenant Signs

Let us look at the various covenants of the covenant of grace to see what signs God appointed for his people and how those signs served to help God's people live in covenant with him.

THE NOAHIC COVENANT

The Noahic covenant was accompanied by the sign of the rainbow.

> And God said, "This is the sign of the covenant that I make between me and you and every living creature that is with you, for all future generations: I have set my bow in the cloud, and it shall be a sign of the covenant between me and the earth. When I bring clouds over the earth and the bow is seen in the clouds, I will remember my covenant that is between me and you and every living creature of all flesh. And the waters shall never again become a flood to destroy all flesh. When the bow is in the clouds, I will see it and remember the everlasting covenant between God and every living creature of all flesh that is on the earth." God said to Noah, "This is the sign of the covenant that I have established between me and all flesh that is on the earth." (Gen. 9:12–17)

God gave the rainbow as "the sign of the covenant" he had made with Noah. The rainbow is fitting as a visible and public sign. By God's appointment, the rainbow calls to mind the covenant that God made to preserve the earth from another catastrophic judgment by flood. Rainbows typically appear when sunlight meets water droplets near the cessation of rain. The rainbow, then, is a natural reminder that God will not destroy the world again by water. The worldwide visibility of the rainbow, furthermore, is appropriate since the preservation of the whole creation is the concern of this covenant.

Interestingly, the rainbow is said here to be a reminder *to God.* God, of course, does not forget and does not need prompting or reminding. His creatures, however, are prone to forget. This expression vividly helps us to grasp the fact that God will never forget and will always be faithful to his covenant promises.

What, then, should come to mind when we behold the rainbow as a covenant sign? We should remember God's promise to Noah not to destroy the world again by water. This sign should confirm that promise to all who look upon the sign in faith. Further, we should remember that God is true to his word. He is not like human beings, who forget or change their minds. He is faithful and will do all that he has said he will do.

THE ABRAHAMIC COVENANT

We have already been introduced to the sign of the Abrahamic covenant, circumcision. What did circumcision mean to Abraham? The apostle Paul helps us to understand its significance.

> [Abraham] received the sign of circumcision as a seal of the righteousness that he had by faith while he was still uncircumcised. The purpose was to make him the father of all who believe without being circumcised, so that righteousness would be counted to them as well, and to make him the father of the circumcised who are not merely circumcised but who also walk in the footsteps of the faith that our father Abraham had before he was circumcised. (Rom. 4:11–12)

Paul here uses two words to describe circumcision—"sign" and "seal." Circumcision is a "sign" in that it visibly represents the promises that God offers his people in covenant with him. In what sense is circumcision a "seal"? "Seals" in the ancient world served to mark ownership and to authenticate an object. Therefore, one who bore the seal of circumcision was set apart by God for himself. He no longer was to be regarded as belonging to the world. Nor did he belong to himself. He belonged to God. More fundamentally, and closer to Paul's meaning in Romans 4, circumcision was a seal of a particular promise ("righteousness by faith"). Abraham, Paul stresses, was a man who *already had* righteousness by faith (see Genesis 12; 15). Circumcision did not convey to Abraham that benefit (Rom. 4:11). Circumcision, rather, confirmed to believing Abraham the benefit that was already his. Circumcision was designed to accompany faith in such a way that faith, helped by what that sign represented to the recipient, would be strengthened by grace. Circumcision did not make Abraham a believer in God, nor did it make him right with God. Circumcision was a means by which God grew and strengthened the justifying faith that Abraham already had while uncircumcised.[1]

Paul tells us here that circumcision was a sign and seal of "righteousness by faith," that is, the grace of justification. Circumcision was a tangible indicator and confirmation that God had declared Abraham righteous in his sight, not because of anything that Abraham had done or would do, but solely on the basis of the righteousness of another. This righteousness was that of the promised offspring. It was "counted," that is, imputed or reckoned to Abraham. Abraham received this imputed righteousness by faith alone.

Abraham put his faith in Christ, but he did not put his faith in the Christ who had already been crucified and raised from the dead.

---

1. Recipients of circumcision did not necessarily possess faith. To all recipients, however, circumcision signified the promise, a promise that could only be received through faith.

Abraham's trust was in the promise of God. The substance of that promise, according to both Moses and Paul, is the offspring (Christ) whom God would raise up from Abraham's own body. This offspring would bring gospel blessing to the nations, specifically, the blessing of *justification* (see Gal. 3:1–14).

Circumcision pointed Abraham to that promise in a striking way. Circumcision was applied to the male procreative organ, the organ by means of which God's promise to Abraham would come into being. There was, then, a fitting connection between the sign of circumcision and the promise signified. Abraham bore in his own body a physical mark intended to direct him to the divine promise to bring into the world the Redeemer of sinners. In so putting faith in God's promise, represented in the sign of circumcision, Abraham had the truth of this promise confirmed to him. Circumcision was to Abraham, therefore, both sign and seal of the covenant promise to justify sinners by the work of Jesus Christ. It was God's appointed means of helping Abraham to grow "strong in his faith" (Rom. 4:20).

Later biblical revelation discloses additional meaning to circumcision. In Deuteronomy, God both commands (Deut. 10:16; cf. Jer. 4:4) and promises (Deut. 30:6) to Israel the circumcision of the heart. Circumcision here refers to a radical work upon the heart, the result of which is single-hearted and dedicated service to the Lord. Paul helps us to understand that this circumcision is not outward but inward, the work of the Holy Spirit (Rom. 2:28–29) on the basis of the work of Christ on the cross (Col. 2:11, 14). This circumcision takes place when a person is brought from spiritual death to spiritual life (Col. 2:11–13). This line of teaching helps us to see that covenant signs can bear multiple and complementary lines of signification. That is to say, a single covenant sign can point observers to more than one covenant promise.

THE MOSAIC COVENANT AND THE NEW COVENANT

The Mosaic covenant has an appointed covenant sign, the Passover meal. I will say more about this sign below and then again in the next chapter. For now, we may briefly take up the signs of the new covenant. When we come to the new covenant, we find that Christ has appointed not one but two covenant signs—baptism and the Lord's Supper. To appreciate these two new covenant signs, we should first explore the two corresponding signs available to Israelites under the old, or Mosaic, covenant.

A male member of the old covenant would have had two primary covenant signs given to him by God. The first was circumcision, administered to him (ordinarily) when he was eight days old. Thus, almost from birth he would have had the sign of the covenant placed upon him. At no point in his conscious existence would he have been without the sign to point him to the covenant promises of God. The second sign, available to men and women, was the Passover meal. This meal annually commemorated God's redemption of Israel from slavery in Egypt. It involved the preparation and consumption of a lamb and the rehearsal of God's goodness in delivering his people from bondage. As a yearly observance, it regularly and consistently put before the Israelites' minds the character of their God and their own identity and calling as his people.

Even as these two signs pointed to the same promise-making God and were intended for the same covenant community, there were some differences between them. Circumcision pointed, as we have seen, to justification by faith alone and to the inner renewal that God alone can perform in a person. Passover uniquely pointed to God's great work of redeeming his people from slavery and for service to him. Circumcision was an initiatory rite, taking place soon after one's birth. Passover was an ongoing rite, to be received and enjoyed every year. In circumcision, the recipient was passive, or acted upon; in Passover, the recipient was active or engaged in a way that he was not in circumcision. Circumcision and Passover each marked out the identity and membership of God's people apart from the world, but they did so in different ways.

Under the new covenant, both circumcision and Passover were discontinued as covenant signs. In their place, under the new covenant, Jesus institutes two new covenant signs: baptism and the Lord's Supper. Baptism corresponds to circumcision; the Lord's Supper corresponds to Passover. The next two chapters will explore correspondences between Passover and the Lord's Supper. Let us now reflect briefly on the similarities and differences between the covenant signs of circumcision and baptism.

Like circumcision, baptism is an initiatory rite, applied to covenant members upon their formal entrance into the covenant community (see Matt. 28:18–20). Like circumcision, in baptism, one is passive—water is applied to the recipient. Unlike circumcision, however, both males and females may receive the covenant sign of baptism. We may point to at least two reasons why this is so. One reason surely has to do with the expansiveness of the new covenant relative to the old. Under the new covenant, the breadth and experiential power of redemptive blessing increases dramatically relative to the old. Covenant blessing now goes out to all nations. Those who receive this blessing do so with greater fullness and clarity of understanding than did their counterparts under the old covenant. Given this character of the new covenant, we are not surprised to see the sphere of the recipients of the initiatory covenant sign broadened in terms of gender.[2]

---

2. There is a sense in which this sphere is broadened with respect to ethnicity as well. Circumcision was typically applied to Jewish men; baptism is applied to all ethnicities. We should note, however, that, under the old covenant, circumcision was not exclusively and by design a

There is another reason for the broadening of the recipients of the initiatory covenant sign. Circumcision was an indicator, we have seen, of the promise of the coming Messiah, the offspring of Abraham who would bring blessing to the nations. In light of that reality, the sign of circumcision was placed upon the male procreative organ. Under the new covenant, however, Christ has come in the flesh. He has completed his work on the basis of which sinners are justified. We await his return, but we rejoice that he has already appeared to save sinners. Because the promised offspring, Christ, has entered history and completed his redemptive work, the initiatory covenant sign is no longer tied to the promise of an offspring yet to be conceived and born. It is therefore understandable why God no longer restricts the application of the initiatory covenant sign to males.

We have reflected on the ways in which circumcision pointed *ahead* to Christ. How does baptism point *back* to Christ? We know that Jesus Christ underwent a kind of water baptism at the hands of John the Baptist at the outset of his own public ministry (Matt. 3:13–17). He submitted to John's baptism as a way of publicly identifying with his people, committing himself to taking on their obligations as sinners. *Baptism*, furthermore, is a word that Jesus used on more than one occasion to describe his ordeal on the cross (Mark 10:38; Luke 12:50). Baptism, in that context, describes what Jesus underwent to pay the penalty for the sins of his people. *Baptism* is also a word that Jesus used to describe the blessings that the Holy Spirit brings upon God's people after Jesus's resurrection and ascension (see Luke 3:16; Acts 1:5; 2:1–4, 17–18).

Baptism, then, denotes the work of Christ for his people. He has undertaken all that sinners need for the demands of righteousness to be met (Matt. 3:15). That work includes his bearing their sins on

---

Jewish rite. God made provision in Genesis 17, as we have seen, for non-Jewish men brought into Abraham's household to be circumcised.

the cross. Because Jesus's experience of baptism was one of curse and judgment, his people's experience of baptism will be one only of blessing. Water baptism points us simultaneously to the judgment that Jesus bore on our behalf and to the redemptive blessing that he pours out upon us by the Holy Spirit. It uniquely points us to Christ and to his finished work on our behalf.[3]

Baptism and circumcision differ, then, in the vantage points or perspectives from which each points to the work of Christ. There is one further way in which circumcision and baptism differ. Circumcision necessarily involved the shedding of the recipient's blood. It was a bloody rite. Baptism, however, is administered by the pouring of water. There is no shedding of the recipient's blood. In that respect, it is a bloodless rite. The finished work of Christ on the cross accounts for this difference between circumcision and baptism. At the cross, Christ shed his blood for sinners. That blood completely pays for all the sins of his people (Col. 2:13–14). Baptism points us, among other things, to the finished work of Christ on the cross. It is fitting that a rite signifying the finished blood sacrifice of Christ would itself be administered bloodlessly. Christ's blood is sufficient.

A Summary of Covenant Signs

Let us summarize what we have seen so far about covenant signs. In each of the various administrations of the covenant of grace, God appointed a covenant sign. He appointed the rainbow to accompany the Noahic covenant, circumcision to accompany the Abrahamic covenant, Passover to accompany the Mosaic covenant, and baptism

---

3. Significantly, to receive the sign of baptism but to remain in unbelief and impenitence is a serious matter. Baptism testifies both to blessing *and* to judgment. Baptism tells us that if we do not trust in Christ as our Savior from sin, then we will have to bear judgment for our sin in our own persons. Baptism is a summons to sinners to find refuge in Christ (the judgment bearer) alone for salvation. Baptism is not mute and does not allow us to remain indifferent to the realities it signifies to us. Circumcision, we may note, functioned in the same way under the Abrahamic and Mosaic covenants.

and the Lord's Supper to accompany the new covenant. We may fairly speak of a pattern in God's covenants with his people. He not only *speaks* his word of blessing to us in his covenants but also *shows* us that same word through covenant signs that are specifically appointed to direct our five senses to the promise and to strengthen and confirm our faith in the promises so signified. Covenant signs are a recurring feature of God's covenants with human beings. They testify to God's desire to draw near to us as whole persons, soul and body. They testify to the faith trials and the temptations to unbelief we experience in this world. They testify to God's condescending kindness to us to provide helps and supports for our faith in the face of those temptations. They testify visibly, sensibly, and concretely to the truth of God's Word. We have many reasons to be grateful to God for appointing these signs for our help and benefit.

Covenants with No Apparent Signs

I have argued for a pattern of signs within God's covenants with humans. There are two covenants in the Bible that, on first glance, appear to break from that pattern. On closer inspection, however, they in fact fit that pattern well.

THE DAVIDIC COVENANT

The first covenant is the Davidic covenant. Scripture does not testify to a sign that uniquely accompanies the Davidic covenant. But the difficulty we face in the absence of such a sign is more apparent than real.

The Davidic covenant is, in reality, an extension and expansion of the Abrahamic covenant. That is, it specifies that the promised offspring of Abraham through whom blessing will come to the nations will be from the line of Abraham's descendant, David. This covenant tells us even more about the identity of this offspring. He will stand in unique relation to God as "son" (2 Sam. 7:14). He will reign from the throne of David, and that reign will never end (2 Sam. 7:12–16). For these reasons, the Davidic covenant is not independent of but closely tied to the Abrahamic covenant. It extends even as it expands the Abrahamic covenant.

This state of affairs likely accounts for the absence of an appointed sign in this covenantal administration. Instead of presenting a brand-new covenant sign, the Davidic covenant invested the existing covenant sign of circumcision with enriched meaning. We have, then, not a new sign instituted but an old sign reinvigorated. In the wake of the Davidic covenant, God's people were to behold the covenant sign of circumcision with a deeper and wider grasp of the promised offspring to whom the sign pointed them. When understood along these lines, the Davidic covenant is not anomalous. It does not present a categorical exception to God's pattern with his people. The absence of a new sign, rather, discloses the true purpose of the Davidic covenant and its organic relationship with the Abrahamic covenant that has preceded it.

The Covenant of Works

The second covenant that seems to lack an accompanying sign is the covenant of works, the covenant that God made with Adam before the fall. We have seen that covenant signs accompany each administration of the covenant of grace. We might expect the same principle to hold for the covenant of works. But it is difficult to identify a clear covenant sign from Scripture's account of this covenant. If we attend to what Scripture says about this covenant, however, we will, in fact, identify a sign that God gave in conjunction with it.

Recall that God made the covenant of works with Adam as a representative person. He stood not only for himself but for all his ordinary descendants. The condition of that covenant was obedience to God's commands, including the particular command not to eat of the tree of knowledge of good and evil. God implicitly pledged to Adam a confirmed and consummate life, provided Adam continued in obedience to him.

We have observed that the special command given to Adam centered on the "tree of the knowledge of good and evil" (Gen. 2:17). But another tree is mentioned in the garden alongside the tree of knowledge of good and evil. It is the "tree of life," and this tree is said to be "in the midst of the garden" (Gen. 2:9). The fact that this tree is given a designated name ("tree of life"), that its name ("life") is tied to the promise of the covenant, and that it is paired with another tree that plays a significant role in the covenant of works prompts us to ask what role this tree may have played in this covenant.

Our suspicion that the tree of life played a role in this covenant is confirmed by something that God said shortly before he exiled Adam and Eve from the garden. In a word of self-deliberation, God said, "'Behold, the man has become like one of us in knowing good and evil. Now lest he reach out his hand and take also of the tree of life and eat, and live forever'—therefore the LORD God sent him out from the garden of Eden to work the ground from which he was taken" (Gen. 3:22–23). This statement is the reason assigned for removing Adam from the garden. God here reasoned that, in light of the fall ("the man has become like one of us in knowing good and evil"), it was singularly inappropriate that Adam, fallen into sin, should then eat of the tree of life. This state of affairs further confirms our suspicion that the tree of life may have played a role in connection with the covenant of works—a covenant that Adam broke by his disobedience.

What role might this be? This tree appears to have served as a pledge or representation of the confirmed and consummate life that God promised Adam for his obedience in the covenant of works.

After all, there is a divinely appointed connection between the eating of that tree and "liv[ing] forever" (Gen. 3:22).

Adam would not, then, have eaten of this tree until "after [the] probation" since it was "the sacramental means for communicating the highest life" held out to Adam in the covenant.[4] That the tree of life played such a role in the covenant of works is confirmed by the reappearance of the tree in the last book of the Bible, Revelation.

> He who has an ear, let him hear what the Spirit say to the churches. To the one who conquers I will grant to eat of the tree of life, which is in the paradise of God. (Rev. 2:7)

> Then the angel showed me the river of the water of life, bright as crystal, flowing from the throne of God and of the Lamb through the middle of the street of the city; also on either side of the river, the tree of life with its twelve kinds of fruit, yielding its fruit each month. The leaves of the tree were for the healing of the nations. (Rev. 22:1–2)

In both passages, the tree of life is held out to believers in Christ. Specifically, it is a future blessing that Christ gives to his people. It is a reward for the believer who perseveres to the end. It is a centerpiece of the celestial city of consummation. The life signified by this tree, then, is consummate life. It is guaranteed to the believer in Christ because Christ has earned that life and given his people certain title to that life. But we have not yet experienced that life in full. We have already and partially begun to experience the life of the age to come, but the consummate experience of that life awaits us.

This state of affairs helps us to see why it was inappropriate for

---

4. Geerhardus Vos, *Biblical Theology* (Edinburgh: Banner of Truth, 1975), 28. What follows is indebted to Vos's observations on 27–29. Throughout church history, Christians have applied the term *sacrament* to baptism and the Lord's Supper. Vos is saying that the tree of life was to function in the way that baptism and the Lord's Supper do for believers today.

fallen Adam to eat of that tree. Because of his sin in eating the forbidden fruit, he no longer had access to the tree of life by the path of covenant obedience. God judicially barred that way to Adam (and to ordinary human beings following him). But Christ, the second Adam, has blazed a trail to that tree for us by his obedience and death.[5] We do not yet eat of that tree, but we will surely eat of that tree when Christ returns. Christ has done what Adam failed to do. He has won for us everlasting life, that is, fellowship and communion with the living God.

Conclusion

The Bible, then, begins and ends with the tree of life. This tree points to the great concern of the Bible—communion with God in the presence of God. For this we were created, and for this we were redeemed. In Adam, we have forfeited our right to that chief blessing. In Christ, we have been given title to that chief blessing.

Significantly, both Genesis and Revelation describe this tree of life as something that human beings eat or consume. At significant moments in the Bible, human beings enjoy a meal with God and are invited to dine at a special table that God has spread for us. It is not surprising, then, to see that God appointed under the Mosaic covenant and under the new covenant distinct meals as covenant signs—the Passover (Mosaic covenant) and the Lord's Supper (new covenant). Such meals capture something that sits at the very heart of covenant life with God. Before we reflect specifically upon the new covenant sign and meal, the Lord's Supper, we will give thought to the pattern of meals that God has provided his people across redemptive history.

---

5. Significantly, the death that gives us access to the tree of life was the death of Christ upon a tree, that is, the cross (Gal. 3:13).

3

Covenant Meals

We have seen that the Bible is a covenantal book, and the Bible's theology is a covenantal theology. Before the fall, God entered into a covenant with Adam (and with us in Adam). Since the fall, God has administered his redemptive promises through a succession of covenants. These covenants build upon one another, extending and expanding the promise of God to save a multitude of sinners, Jew and Gentile, by the work of his Son, our covenant Head, Jesus Christ.

We have also seen that God has appointed signs within these covenants. These signs represent to the five senses the gospel realities administered in God's gracious covenants. God gives us such representations in order to help strengthen our faith. Two of these signs are Passover and the Lord's Supper. God gave the Passover to his people as a sign of the Mosaic covenant, and the Lord's Supper to his people as a sign of the new covenant.

These two signs are meals. It is not accidental that God gave his people covenant signs in this form. Recall that the Bible begins and ends with the "tree of life." The significance of the tree of life in both Genesis and Revelation is the same. In each it represents consummate fellowship with God in his very presence. In between these two trees, we see a sequence of meals representing who God is and what he does for his people.

Since Passover and the Lord's Supper fall within that sequence, we will look more carefully at the succession of meals within redemptive history. We will see themes and trends that will help us better appreciate the Lord's Supper when we look at it in the next chapter. We may look at the meals of Scripture under three historical and canonical headings—the Pentateuch, the Prophets, and the New Testament.

The Pentateuch

When God redeemed Israel from Egypt, he instituted a cycle of feasts designed to structure Israel's year. The goal of these feasts was to reinforce central lessons about who God was and what he had done for Israel. These feasts afforded God's delivered people the opportunity to respond to him appropriately.

The feasts are described together in both Leviticus 23 and Deuteronomy 16. In Leviticus 23, God describes seven feasts that ran the course of a calendar year and were to be part of the annual cycle of Israel's worship (23:2, 4).

The Feast of Passover. The first feast was that of Passover, immediately followed by the Feast of Unleavened Bread (Lev. 23:5–6). Passover lasted a single day; Unleavened Bread, seven days. What was the significance of each of these festivals? Passover commemorated the Lord's deliverance of Israel from bondage in Egypt (see Ex. 12:1–28, 43–49). On the eve of the exodus, God commanded Israel to prepare to kill a Passover lamb at twilight (Ex. 12:6, 21).[1] The Israelites were to do two things with that lamb. First, they were to apply the blood of the lamb to the "doorposts

---

1. Israel's days began and ended at sunset. Twilight, then, marked the beginning of a new day, in this case, the day of Passover.

and the lintel of the houses in which they [would] eat it" (Ex. 12:7). The blood would serve as a "sign": "When I see the blood," God said, "I will pass over you, and no plague will befall you to destroy you, when I strike the land of Egypt" (Ex. 12:13; cf. 12:23). God was going to strike the firstborn of Egypt, but not the firstborn of Israel. Instead, God passed over the homes of the Israelites, sparing their children from the judgment of death. For this reason, God laid special claim to the firstborn of the Israelites (Ex. 13:2) and pronounced them "redeemed" (Ex. 13:13, 15).

God was teaching Israel an important lesson. The people themselves deserved judgment. God, however, did not give them what they deserved. But God's mercy to Israel came at great cost. A substitute had to die in order that Israel might live. God did execute judgment upon Israel, but that judgment did not fall upon the Israelites. It fell upon the sacrificial lamb that God had appointed to die in their place. In this way, the New Testament writers tell us, God was preparing Israel for the sacrificial and substitutionary death of God's own Son, Jesus Christ, who bore in his own body on the cross the curse that sinners deserve (John 1:29; 1 Cor. 5:7; Gal. 3:13). Jesus did this in order that we might, through faith in him, find forgiveness and acceptance in his name (Rom. 3:21–26; Col. 2:12–13).

The second thing that God commanded Israel to do with the sacrificial lamb was to eat it (Ex. 12:7–11). God gave the Israelites some very specific instructions about how they were to eat that lamb. It was to be cooked in a certain way (Ex. 12:8–9). They were to eat it on the night of the Passover and destroy whatever remained before morning (Ex. 12:10). They were to eat it "with [their] belt fastened, . . . sandals on [their] feet, and . . . staff in [their hand]," that is, in haste (Ex. 12:11). These instructions reinforced the character of the meal as commemorative of the Lord's rescue and deliverance of Israel in the exodus.

The meal was also to be a communal meal. In Exodus, God commands that the lamb be eaten by the household (Ex. 12:4). All

Israel was to sacrifice the lamb at the same time (Ex. 12:6). In Deuteronomy, envisioning the day when Israel would take up residence in the Promised Land, God commands Israel to eat the lamb "at the place that the Lord your God will choose, to make his name dwell in it," that is, the city of Jerusalem (Deut. 16:6). Not only were Israelites to eat the Passover meal in community, but they were also instructed to eat it in the presence of God. In the Passover meal, God was assembling his people each year to enjoy a meal in his presence.

The Feast of Unleavened Bread. Closely related to the Feast of Passover was the Feast of Unleavened Bread. This feast ran a full week and began and ended with "holy convocations," days on which the people of Israel would lay down their "ordinary work" and gather for worship in the presence of the Lord (Lev. 23:4, 8). On each of these days, Israel was to "present a food offering to the Lord" and was herself to "eat unleavened bread" (Lev. 23:6, 8). The command to eat unleavened bread was accompanied by a command that the Israelites remove leaven from their houses (Ex. 12:15, 19; Deut. 16:4). Because the Passover lamb was to be eaten with unleavened bread, the command to eat unleavened bread for the week *following* Passover was probably intended to help Israel keep in mind her deliverance in the exodus (Ex. 12:8, cf. 12:34, 39). The New Testament writers sometimes speak of leaven as a metaphor for the sin that God's redeemed people are to put away (see Mark 8:15; 1 Cor. 5:6). This connection reinforces the calling of God's people to be a holy people, set apart from bondage to sin and for the Lord and the liberty of his service.

The Feast of Firstfruits and the Feast of Weeks. Following Passover and Unleavened Bread were two additional feasts. The Feast of Firstfruits and the Feast of Weeks (Lev. 23:9–14, 15–22) commemorated the Lord's bountiful provision in Israel's harvests. Israel was to begin observing the

Feast of Firstfruits upon arriving in the land. This feast would commemorate the Lord's bountiful provision in the spring harvest. The "firstfruits of [the] harvest" were to be brought to the priest, who presented them to the Lord, along with sacrifices, one of which is described as "a food offering to the LORD with a pleasing aroma" (Lev. 23:10, 13). The Feast of Weeks was observed "seven full weeks from the day after the Sabbath, from the day that you brought the sheaf of the wave offering . . . fifty days to the day after the seventh Sabbath" (Lev. 23:15–16). This feast involved the presentation of several types of offerings to the Lord. The feast was to be a "holy convocation," a day set apart for the public worship of God (Lev. 23:8, 11–12). Insofar as the day commemorated the bountiful provision of the Lord, it was to be characterized by corporate joy, the joy of a people who had once been "slave[s] in Egypt" (Deut. 16:10–12).

The Feast of Weeks had an important social dimension to it. God commanded Israel to leave a portion of the harvest "for the poor and for the sojourner" (Lev. 23:22). God appointed "the sojourner, the fatherless, and the widow who are among you" to come to Jerusalem for the joyful celebration of this feast (Deut. 16:11). God intended for all his people to share in the joy of that occasion. For that reason, God commanded his people to ensure that the outliers and needy in Israel not be excluded either from the blessings that he had poured out upon his people or from the joyful celebration of the God who had provided those blessings.[2]

The Feast of Trumpets, the Day of Atonement, and the Feast of Booths. The final three feasts were all observed within fifteen days of each other. The Feast of Trumpets was "a day of solemn rest, a memorial proclaimed with blast of trumpets, a holy convocation," on which

---

2. Significantly, the day of Pentecost (Acts 2) coincides with the Feast of Weeks (the Greek word *pentēkostē*, from which we get *Pentecost*, means "fiftieth"; see Lev. 23:16). Pentecost is the Father's gracious and bountiful provision, through the exalted Son, of the Spirit to the church. As Peter stresses in his explanatory sermon, this provision brings to fulfillment the prophecy of Joel 2, in which God said, "I will pour out my Spirit on all flesh" (Acts 2:17, citing Joel 2:28).

Israel "present[ed] a food offering to the LORD" (Lev. 23:24–25). The Day of Atonement was characterized by "afflict[ion]" (Lev. 23:27, 29, 32). It was an annual occasion for Israel "to make atonement for [them] before the LORD [their] God" (Lev. 23:28). Israel congregated in holy assembly in order to remember and repent of sin for which they sought the Lord's mercy.

If the Day of Atonement was marked by solemnity, the Feast of Booths, just five days later, was marked by joy. Like the Day of Atonement, the Feast of Booths was to be observed by "holy convocation" and "food offerings" (Lev. 23:35–36). But the Feast of Booths, which lasted eight days, was to be characterized by joy before the Lord, the God of Israel (Lev. 23:40). Specifically, this feast commemorated Israel's wilderness wanderings and the Lord's provision and care for Israel in the wilderness (Lev. 23:42–43). It also commemorated the Lord's provision in the fall harvest (Deut. 16:13, 15).

———

Israel was to observe these seven feasts every year without interruption. God was teaching Israel several lessons through this annual cycle of feasts. First, he was providing his people with ongoing reminders of his covenantal mercies and faithfulness to them. God's power and mercy in the exodus, God's faithfulness to provide in the wilderness, and God's bountiful provision in the land were all visibly and symbolically set before Israel year after year. Second, God was calling his people to draw near into his presence on regular occasions. These feasts were occasions of worship, when the people of God would seek and find blessing from nearness to their Redeemer. Third, these feasts were corporate. In them, God was summoning Israel to worship him not privately but in the company of his covenant people. Consequently, the Israelites could not be indifferent to the needs and wants of the least in their number. God intended the bounty of the land to benefit the whole covenant community, without regard to wealth or status. Fourth, these feasts called forth a range of affections appropriate for life in covenant with God. Sometimes feasts called Israel to mourn for sin. On other occasions, God commanded his people to be "altogether joyful" in view of his goodness (Deut. 16:15). Fifth and finally, these feasts all centered on food. Israel was commanded not only to bring various offerings before the Lord but also to partake of some of those offerings in the presence of the Lord. What made these meals special was not merely that they were occasional or prepared to specification, but that they were eaten with and in the presence of the Lord.

What the feasts that God instituted in the Law of Moses were supposed to teach Israel is powerfully captured in the well-known Twenty-Third Psalm, which David penned for the congregation of Israel to sing to God's praise. The psalm as a whole celebrates the ways in which God cares for his people as their Shepherd (23:1). David closes the psalm by reflecting on the Lord's faithful and bountiful provision.

> You prepare a table before me
>   in the presence of my enemies;
> you anoint my head with oil;
>   my cup overflows.
> Surely goodness and mercy shall follow me
>   all the days of my life,
> and I shall dwell in the house of the LORD
>   forever. (23:5–6)

Even though David is not beyond the reach of his enemies, his mind is not consumed with his enemies. His mind, rather, turns to his Shepherd. God has set a table for David and has bountifully provided for him at that table.

> You anoint my head with oil;
>> my cup overflows.

This table presents the abiding, abundant "goodness and mercy" of the Lord to David. This goodness and mercy comes to expression in David's nearness to his God: "I shall dwell in the house of the LORD forever." God, in covenant mercy, has brought David near to him in mercy and for fellowship. The feast cycle of the Law reinforced this basic truth of the covenant for Israel every year. The God who had redeemed Israel and taken her into covenant had never failed and would certainly continue to provide abundantly for her. The highest blessing that God could and did give Israel was himself. Near to God, Israel would know the blessing of fellowship and communion in his presence, and from that chief blessing would flow every other blessing that God graciously gave to his people.

The Prophets

In the Law, God taught Israel important lessons about life in covenant with him. One of the teaching tools that he provided in the Law was the annual cycle of feasts. The focal point of these feasts was the covenant meals that God appointed Israel to enjoy in his presence. These feasts reinforced an important principle in God's dealings with his old covenant people. The physical or material blessings that Israel enjoyed from the Lord were never ends in themselves. They were always designed to point beyond themselves to the spiritual blessings that God provided in covenant with his people. For Israel, they were to be the occasions and even means by which God's people would come to experience the eternal blessings that God supplied through the work of his Son.[3]

For this reason, God frequently appealed to feasts, meals, and

---

3. This is a point that Jesus powerfully makes in his discourse in John 6. He rebukes the Israelites of his day for failing to see that the bread that God supplied through Moses in the wilderness pointed beyond itself to Jesus, "the living bread that came down from heaven," who brings eternal life to those who feed upon him by faith (John 6:51).

food in speaking to his people through the Prophets. We may look at the teaching of the Prophets in this regard along three lines: displeasure, curse, and restoration.

DISPLEASURE

First, God expressed his displeasure for his people's covenant treachery in terms of the covenant meals that he had instituted in the Law. Consider two examples.

The first comes from the opening chapter of Isaiah, which is a searing indictment of Israel. They are a

> sinful nation,
>> a people laden with iniquity. . . .
> They have forsaken the LORD,
>> they have despised the Holy One of Israel. . . .
>
> The whole head is sick,
>> and the whole heart faint.
> From the sole of the foot even to the head,
>> there is no soundness in it. (Isa. 1:4–6)

What particularly grieves the Lord is their ceremonial scrupulousness coupled with their moral depravity.

> What to me is the multitude of your sacrifices?
>> says the LORD;
> I have had enough of burnt offerings of rams
>> and the fat of well-fed beasts;
> I do not delight in the blood of bulls,
>> or of lambs, or of goats.
>
> When you come to appear before me,
>> who has required of you
>> this trampling of my courts?

> Bring no more vain offerings;
>> incense is an abomination to me.
> New moon and Sabbath and the calling of convocations—
>> I cannot endure iniquity and solemn assembly.
> Your new moons and your appointed feasts
>> my soul hates;
> they have become a burden to me;
>> I am weary of bearing them. (Isa. 1:11–14)

The fact that Israel maintains ritual precision while cherishing "iniquity" renders the feasts a "burden" to the Lord. This disconnect utterly corrupts the purpose of the feasts that God gave his people, namely, to foster trust, devotion, and obedience to the Lord. God tells the Israelites that they must address their moral problem if the feasts are to be acceptable in his sight (see Isa. 1:16–17).

The second example comes from the prophet Amos, through whom God makes a similar point.

> I hate, I despise your feasts,
>> and I take no delight in your solemn assemblies.
> Even though you offer me your burnt offerings and grain
>>> offerings,
>> I will not accept them;
> and the peace offerings of your fattened animals,
>> I will not look upon them.
> Take away from me the noise of your songs;
>> to the melody of your harps I will not listen.
> But let justice roll down like waters,
>> and righteousness like an ever-flowing stream.
>>> (Amos 5:21–24)

God expresses in the strongest terms his displeasure in Israel's "assemblies," "offerings," and musical expressions of praise. The reason for his displeasure is given in the remedy—Israel must commit itself to the pursuit of "justice" and "righteousness." The people's injustice and moral depravity renders their observation of the Law's feasts a stench in the Lord's nostrils.

CURSE

A second line of the Prophets' teaching is that the curses of the covenant will fall upon a disobedient people precisely in terms of food. If food and feasting are the ways in which the Lord expresses and conveys covenant blessing, their removal and absence will be how he will express and convey covenant curse. This point is underscored by the Lord in Deuteronomy 32, the "Song of Witness." Because Israel will forsake God in the pursuit of idols (32:21), God will visit them with "hunger . . . plague and . . . pestilence" (32:24). Centuries later, the prophet Jeremiah will declare that "famine" will be among the curses that come upon Israel for having broken the covenant (Jer. 11:10, 22). Even "though they offer burnt offering and grain offering," God says through Jeremiah, "I will not accept them. But I will consume them by the sword, by famine, and by pestilence" (Jer. 14:12). In a tragic irony, when covenant breakers attempt to draw near to God through the system of covenant meals that he has instituted, he will judge them by removing food from them.

RESTORATION

A third line of the Prophets' teaching concerns the restoration that God pledges to bring about for his people. If God threatens and enacts covenant curse in the realm of food and meal, then covenant restoration will take the form of food and meal as well. We may point to two of many examples of this promise from among the Prophets.

In Isaiah 25, God promises to gather the nations for a feast that he has prepared for them.

> On this mountain the Lord of hosts will make for all
>> peoples
>> a feast of rich food, a feast of well-aged wine,
>> of rich food full of marrow, of aged wine well refined.
> And he will swallow up on this mountain
>> the covering that is cast over all peoples,
>> the veil that is spread over all nations.
>> He will swallow up death forever;
> and the Lord God will wipe away tears from all faces,
>> and the reproach of his people he will take away from all
>>> the earth,
>> for the Lord has spoken.
> It will be said on that day,
>> "Behold, this is our God; we have waited for him, that he
>>> might save us.
>> This is the Lord; we have waited for him;
>> let us be glad and rejoice in his salvation." (25:6–9)

God makes a number of remarkable promises in this prophecy. He pledges to gather "all peoples" to "this mountain," that is, "Zion" or "the mountain of the Lord" (Isa. 2:3). This ingathering, Isaiah tells us elsewhere, will happen "in the latter days" (Isa. 2:2). This is, then, an eschatological prophecy, a prophecy concerning the consummation of redemptive history. When God gathers the nations, he does so not for their destruction but for their "salvation" (Isa. 25:9). They will call upon him as "our God." When God gathers the nations to himself for salvation, he will do two things. First, he will remove death, sorrow ("tears"), and the "reproach" of Israel (Isa. 25:8). God will, in other words, do away with the consequences and effects of sin and the curse. Second, God will spread a banquet for his people,

> a feast of rich food, a feast of well-aged wine,
>
> of rich food full of marrow, of aged wine well refined.
>
>> (Isa. 25:6)

The promise of abundant food and wine indicates that God will draw near to the nations in covenant blessing. In drawing near to God, the nations will enjoy spiritual communion and fellowship with him.

How will these realities come to pass? Throughout his prophecy, Isaiah points to the work of God's Servant, upon whom the Spirit will dwell in fullness (see Isa. 11:1–9; 42:1). God will make him

> a covenant for the people,
>
> a light for the nations. (Isa. 42:6: cf. 49:8)

He will bring salvation to the nations because he himself will endure the punishment sinners deserve (see Isa. 52:13–53:12). As a result, "many" people will be "accounted righteous" and the "portion" that God gives him "he shall divide" with his people (Isa. 53:11–12).

This Servant is, of course, the Lord Jesus Christ (Matt. 12:15–21). By his obedience and death, he has paid the full penalty for the sins of his people and won eternal life for them. The bounty of which Isaiah speaks in Isaiah 25 has become reality for the people of God through faith in Christ. We will ultimately and completely experience these realities at our own bodily resurrection when, Paul says, quoting this prophecy, "Death is swallowed up in victory" (1 Cor. 15:54). Even though we await the full realization of this promise in our own lives, we now give "thanks . . . to God, who gives us the victory through our Lord Jesus Christ" (1 Cor. 15:57).

We find a second such promise along these lines in Joel 2:18–32. In this prophecy, Joel speaks about the restoration that God will provide to Israel after the impending judgment of exile.

Then the Lord became jealous for his land
     and had pity on his people.
The Lord answered and said to his people,
"Behold I am sending to you
     grain, wine, and oil,
     and you will be satisfied;
and I will no more make you
     a reproach among the nations. . . .

"Fear not, O land;
     be glad and rejoice,
     for the Lord has done great things!
Fear not, you beasts of the field,
     for the pastures of the wilderness are green;
the tree bears its fruit;
     the fig tree and vine give their full yield.

"Be glad, O children of Zion,
     and rejoice in the Lord your God,
for he has given the early rain for your vindication;
     he has poured down for you abundant rain,
     the early and the latter rain as before.

"The threshing floors shall be full of grain;
     the vats shall overflow with wine and oil.
I will restore to you the years
     that the swarming locust has eaten. . . .

"You shall eat in plenty and be satisfied,
     and praise the name of the Lord your God,
     who has dealt wondrously with you.
And my people shall never again be put to shame.

You shall know that I am in the midst of Israel,

and that I am the LORD your God and there is none else.

And my people shall never again be put to shame." (2:18–19,
     21–25a, 26–27)

In these verses, God is promising to Israel full restoration of bounty in the land. He does so in terms of green pastures, fruit-bearing trees, and bountifully yielding vines (Joel 2:22). In this way, Israel will have an overwhelming supply of grain, wine, and oil (2:24). God will, in fact, restore in blessing what he has removed in curse (2:25a).

What is the underlying significance of this bounty of food and wine? God has removed the "shame" and "reproach" of his people and brought them "vindication" (2:19, 23, 27). He has removed "fear" and brought joy to his people (2:21, 23), even satisfaction (2:26). All of these realities stem from the presence of God in the midst of his people as their covenant God (2:27).

The New Testament helps us to understand these realities in light of their fulfillment in Christ. The apostle Peter, on the day of Pentecost, quotes the verses immediately following this prophecy (Joel 2:28–32). These verses, Peter explains, speak of the outpouring of the Holy Spirit by the Father and the exalted, vindicated Son of God (see Acts 2:16–21, 33). The Father and the Son have poured out the Spirit "on all flesh" so that "everyone who calls on the name of the LORD shall be saved" (Joel 2:28, 32). The saving ministry of Christ, by the Spirit, is available to all kinds of people, without regard to ethnicity. Any who puts his trust in Christ will be saved.

The fact that Joel 2:28–32 follows immediately on Joel 2:19–27 tells us something about the promises of verses 19–27. The promises of bountiful grain, fruit, and wine all refer to the abundant life that Christ has won for sinners in his death and resurrection and now freely gives by the ministry of the Holy Spirit. Joel is speaking, the New Testament writers tell us, of the bountiful life that is enjoyed in union and communion with God the Father, God the Son, and God the Spirit.

Before we leave our study of the promises of restoration, we should also note that the Prophets speak of restoration in terms of renewed observance of the feasts appointed by the Mosaic law. In Zechariah 14, the prophet looks to a day when "the LORD will be king over all the earth" (14:9). On that day, after a great, worldwide battle, the nations will stream to Jerusalem.

> Then everyone who survives of all the nations that have come against Jerusalem shall go up year after year to worship the King, the LORD of hosts, and to keep the Feast of Booths. . . .
>
> And on that day there shall be inscribed on the bells of the horses, "Holy to the LORD." And the pots in the house of the LORD shall be as the bowls before the altar. And every pot in Jerusalem and Judah shall be holy to the LORD of hosts, so that all who sacrifice may come and take of them and boil the meat of the sacrifice in them. And there shall no longer be a trader in the house of the LORD of hosts on that day. (14:16, 20–21)

The nations will come to Jerusalem in order to worship the Lord. They will worship him by keeping the Feast of Booths, a feast, as we have seen, characterized by a joyful sense of the abundance of the Lord's provision. What marks this occasion is the prevalence of holiness. The common implements not only of the temple but also of the city and of the land will be holy (14:20–21). So single-minded will be the people's devotion to the Lord that there will be no mercantile activity in the eschatological temple (14:21).

In Ezekiel 38–39, the prophet Ezekiel describes a great and final battle in which God executes judgment against his enemies from among the nations. After this description, God declares, "I will restore the fortunes of Jacob and have mercy on the whole house of Israel, and I will be jealous for my holy name" (39:25). God will bring them back to the land, will be present with them, and will "pour out [his] Spirit upon [them]" (39:26, 29). The next nine chapters (Ezekiel 40–48) detail an eschatological temple. They detail the layout of the temple, the temple furniture, the temple sacrifices, and the priests' duties in ministering at the temple. In these chapters, God makes provision for the observance of "all the appointed feasts of the house of Israel," including Passover (45:17, 21). The wealth of details in these chapters is overwhelming, but their basic point is captured in the very last verse of the book: "And the name of the city from that time shall be, 'The LORD Is There'" (48:35). God is communicating, in terms and categories familiar to his old covenant people, the way in which he will be present to them in the latter days.

When Zechariah and Ezekiel speak of the observance of the Feasts of Tabernacles and Passover in the latter days, we may ask, should Christians under the new covenant observe these old covenant feasts now or even prepare to observe them in the future? The New Testament's answer to this question is no. The New Testament tells us how these feasts find their intended fulfillment in the person and work of Jesus Christ.

The New Testament

Jesus Christ is the Servant to whom the Prophets looked. As God incarnate, Jesus fulfills God's pledge to dwell with his people in the latter days (see John 1:1–18). He is the one of whom Moses wrote (John 5:46), whose day Abraham rejoiced to see (John 8:56), and whose glory Isaiah beheld in the throne room of God (John 12:41).

How, then, would Jesus have us understand his relationship with the Law and the Prophets?

At the outset of his public ministry, Jesus announces that he has come not to abolish the Law and the Prophets, but to fulfill them (Matt. 5:17). He insists that "until heaven and earth pass away, not an iota, not a dot, will pass away from the Law *until all is accomplished*" (Matt. 5:18). This accomplishment takes place in the redemptive work that Christ came to do. In light of Jesus's life, death, and resurrection, then, his disciples will not keep the law in exactly the same way that God's people under the old covenant did. To take one example, the finished work of Jesus Christ in his death and resurrection means that the old covenant ceremonial system of worship has come to its intended conclusion (Mark 7:19). The ceremonies of old were the "shadow of the things to come," namely, "Christ" their "substance" (Col. 2:17).

Jesus, however, does not cavalierly dismiss or disregard the old covenant system of worship. Rather, in John's Gospel, he shows in the course of his public ministry how this system purposefully foreshadows the work that he has come to do as Messiah and Redeemer. In the Synoptic Gospels (Matthew, Mark, and Luke), furthermore, Jesus situates the kingdom in the context of the unfolding covenants and covenant meals of redemptive history. He does so by speaking of the presence and coming of the kingdom in terms of a grand meal or banquet between God and his people. We may look at Jesus's teaching in John and the Synoptics in turn.

JOHN

From the very beginning of his Gospel, John shows us how Jesus is the fulfillment of the old covenant temple system. In the prologue to his Gospel, John tells us, "The Word became flesh and dwelt among us" (John 1:14). The word "dwelt" could be translated "tabernacled."

The tabernacle of old, John says, pointed to the incarnation. As God dwelt with Israel in a tent (and later the temple), now God has come to abide permanently with his people in the humanity of Jesus Christ. Later in this opening chapter, John the Baptist points to Jesus as "the Lamb of God, who takes away the sin of the world" (John 1:29, 36). Likely, John the Baptist intends to identify Jesus as the Passover sacrifice to whom all the Passover lambs of old pointed. His once-for-all sacrifice on the cross will pay for the sins of people from around the world.

In John 2, John presents two scenes from the beginning of Jesus's earthly ministry. These scenes serve to set the stage for John's account of Jesus's ministry in the rest of the Gospel.

The first scene is the wedding at Cana, where Jesus miraculously turns water into wine (John 2:1–12). Jesus not only performs this miracle but, in so doing, provides wine in abundant quantity and unsurpassed quality (2:6–7, 10). Readers of the Old Testament cannot but pick up what Jesus is saying in this first miraculous "sign" of his (2:11). Wine was among the blessings that God promised to provide in abundance for his old covenant people at the eschatological feast that he would prepare for them. At Cana, Jesus declares that he is the one who supplies that promised wine to his people. Wine is, of course, a picture of the abundant, eternal life that is found in Christ alone. This passage also hints at what it would cost Jesus to provide that wine. He tells his mother, "My hour has not yet come" (2:4). As we read later in John's Gospel, we learn that Jesus's "hour" refers to his death and resurrection. Even on this celebratory occasion, marked by joy and plenty, Jesus reminds us that he must die the accursed death of the cross for last-days blessing to flow to his people.

The second scene places Jesus at the temple in Jerusalem (John 2:13–22). After a display of unparalleled authority in the temple, which he calls his "Father's house" (2:16), Jesus is asked by the Jewish authorities, "What sign do you show us for doing these things?" (2:18). His answer is, "Destroy this temple, and in three days I will raise it up" (2:19). The Jewish authorities mistakenly think that Jesus is talking about the physical temple in Jerusalem. But, John tells us parenthetically, "he was speaking about the temple of his body" (2:21). Jesus is not only prophesying his death and resurrection but also saying something important about the Jerusalem temple in relation to himself. The temple is a symbolic and material pointer to a deeper and lasting reality, namely, the presence of God with human beings in the person of the Lord Jesus Christ. At the resurrection, the Jerusalem temple will have come to its appointed end in redemptive history. From that point forward, we will find the temple in the risen Christ and his people, the church (see Eph. 2:11–22).

If the temple points to Jesus, then all that is associated with the temple points to Jesus as well. This fact helps us to appreciate Jesus's presence at various Jewish feasts in John's narrative. He is present at Tabernacles (John 7–9); Passover (John 2; 5–6; 12–19); and the extrabiblical Feast of Dedication, commemorating the Maccabees' reclaiming and purification of the temple after Syrian occupation and defilement in the second century BC (John 10). Thus, John invites us in these connections to consider how these feasts point to Jesus Christ, and how richly they find their fulfillment in him. Jesus provides in abundance that water and light to which Tabernacles looked forward (John 7:37–39; 8:12). Jesus is both the Bread of Life, the "bread of God . . . who comes down from heaven and gives life to the world" (John 6:33), and the "Lamb of God" (John 1:29; 19:36)—to each of which Passover looked forward. Jesus is the one consecrated of God, the one of whom the temple consecrated by the Maccabees was but a foreshadow (John 10:22, 36).

Jesus, then, is the fulfillment of the whole temple system, including its feasts. He is the ultimate temple into whom his new covenant people, Jew and Gentile, are incorporated by the Spirit and through faith. He is better than Moses and so provides not "the food that perishes" but "the food that endures to eternal life, which the Son of Man will give to [them]" (John 6:27). What exactly does Jesus provide? He provides "bread . . . for the life of the world," namely, "[his] flesh" (John 6:51), and "his blood" to drink (John 6:53). If one "feeds on [his] flesh and drinks [his] blood," he will have "eternal life" and will "abide in [Christ] and [Christ] in him," and Christ "will raise him up on the last day" (6:54, 56). Jesus is not speaking here of cannibalism, as some of his first hearers suspected (John 6:52). Nor is he speaking directly of the Lord's Supper, which he has yet to institute among his disciples.[4] He is speaking of the gift of "eternal life"—that is, receiving and communing with Jesus by faith (John 6:29, 40). By this feeding and drinking faith in Christ, we receive the eternal life that Christ alone provides, a life that endures beyond the grave, and a life that, even now, is "abundant" (John 10:10). These are the realities to which the feasts of the old covenant pointed, and these are the realities in the possession and enjoyment of everyone who believes in Jesus Christ.

Before we leave John's Gospel, we may note that, just as Jesus commenced his public ministry in John at a wedding, John tells us in another place that history will conclude with a wedding feast, namely, "the marriage supper of the Lamb" (Rev. 19:9; cf. 21:2, 9). When Christ returns, he will bring to consummation his people's experience of the life and salvation he has won for them. The image he uses to describe this fullness of life and blessing is a great wedding feast. Jesus Christ is the one who spreads the table for us, who bids us to come and eat, and who provides the meal. He does this for us now and will do this for us at his return.

---

4. And yet, we shall see, Jesus's teaching in this chapter helps us to understand the meaning and significance of the Lord's Supper.

THE SYNOPTIC GOSPELS

What characterizes the Synoptic Gospels (Matthew, Mark, and Luke) and helps to distinguish them from John's Gospel is the way in which they call our attention to Jesus's teaching about the kingdom of God.[5] All three of the Synoptic Gospels document Jesus's beginning his public ministry in Galilee by proclaiming the arrival of the kingdom. For example, "The time is fulfilled, and the kingdom of God is at hand; repent and believe in the gospel" (Mark 1:15). All of Jesus's instruction, parables, and miracles in these Gospel accounts point in some way to the kingdom.

What is the kingdom of God? The kingdom is the redemptive rule and reign of the Lord Jesus Christ. By his life, death, and resurrection, Jesus ushers into history a new order. Redeemed sinners are brought into this order, and they gladly place themselves under the lordship of their Creator and Redeemer.[6] Sinners are saved *from* the tyrannical rule of Satan, by the death and resurrection of the Messiah, and *for* participation and life in the kingdom over which Jesus presides.

Since the kingdom of God not only succeeds the Law and the Prophets but also brings to fulfillment the realities of which they had spoken to Israel (Matt. 11:11–13; 13:51–52), it is not surprising to learn that Jesus speaks of the kingdom in terms of a great meal or banquet that God sets for his people. We may look at a handful of passages in which Jesus helps us to understand the kingdom along these lines.

Early in his ministry, Jesus commends the faith of a Gentile cen-

---

5. This is not to say that John's Gospel ignores the kingdom of God in Jesus's teaching. It does not (see John 3:3, 5; 18:36). It is to say, however, that the word *kingdom* appears only infrequently in John. The same gospel realities to which *kingdom* refers in the Synoptic Gospels appear to us in John under different terms.

6. And yet, as Jesus teaches in many places, some who are outwardly in the kingdom are not truly or inwardly members of the kingdom (see, for example, Matt. 13:47–50).

turion who asks Jesus to heal his servant: "Truly, I tell you, with no one in Israel have I found such faith" (Matt. 8:10). This expression of Gentile faith, unparalleled in Israel, prompts Jesus to speak about Gentiles and Jews in the kingdom of God. "I tell you, many will come from east and west and recline at table with Abraham, Isaac, and Jacob in the kingdom of heaven, while the sons of the kingdom will be thrown into the outer darkness. In that place there will be weeping and gnashing of teeth" (Matt. 8:11–12). Jesus is making three crucial claims about the kingdom here.

First, he describes its panethnic character. There will be both Jews ("Abraham, Isaac, and Jacob"; the parallel passage in Luke adds "prophets," Luke 13:28) and Gentiles ("many will come from east and west"; the parallel passage in Luke adds "and from north and south") participating in the "kingdom of heaven."

Second, Jesus says that "the sons of the kingdom," who are Jews, will be cast out of the kingdom "into the outer darkness," that is, the place of eternal punishment (in Luke's account, Jesus says that "you yourselves [will be] cast out," Luke 13:28). This will happen because they have not put their trust in Jesus, God's Messiah and the kingdom's King. It is not genealogy but faith that settles one's place in the kingdom of God. This is not a brand-new principle. Abraham, Isaac, and Jacob have their place in the kingdom not by virtue of descent but as those who put their trust in God and his Messiah.

Third, and most importantly for our purposes, Jesus describes the kingdom as a great meal that God has provided for his people. Jew and Gentile will "recline at table" together. The kingdom is an order or state of affairs in which God draws near to his people to commune with them. He will provide an abundant spiritual feast. What the Law and the Prophets anticipated, Jesus describes here as dawning and becoming a reality through his person and work.

Jesus tells two parables that portray the kingdom of God as a great wedding banquet (Matt. 22:1–14; Luke 14:7–11). Luke's parable is designed to show how, in the kingdom of God, the one "who exalts himself will be humbled," and the one "who humbles himself will be exalted" (Luke 14:11). Jesus makes this point by describing someone who takes the "lowest place" at a wedding feast and is invited by the host in the presence of all the guests to sit in a more exalted place (Luke 14:10). In a similar fashion, Jesus tells of the humiliation of a guest who takes a prominent seat for himself and is told by the host, in the presence of all the guests, to yield that seat to another person (Luke 14:9). The lesson that Jesus presses in this parable assumes that the kingdom of God should be understood as a great wedding banquet.

In Matthew, Jesus compares the kingdom to a wedding feast but does so in order to make a different point. The gospel offer is represented as a royal invitation to a wedding feast (Matt. 22:2–3). This invitation makes clear that a grand banquet has been prepared for the guests: "Tell those who are invited, 'See, I have prepared my dinner, my oxen and my fat calves have been slaughtered, and everything is ready. Come to the wedding feast'" (Matt. 22:4).

Jesus's parable is a veiled description of the Jewish people's rejection of Christ and the resulting extension of the gospel to the nations (Matt. 22:8–9). Jesus also stresses that merely responding to the invitation is not enough. One must put his faith in Christ and follow him as his disciple (see Matt. 22:11–14).

In this parable, and in keeping with the Prophets, Jesus speaks of latter-day blessing as a feast that God has prepared for his people. This parable shows how the coming of the kingdom, the offer of the gospel, and the person and work of Jesus Christ should all be understood in terms of the image of a great banquet. The gospel is a wedding invitation that calls sinners to feast on the rich food that God has provided for people in the life, death, and resurrection of the Lord Jesus Christ.

We may briefly mention two other passages in which Jesus speaks of the kingdom as a great marriage feast. The parable of the ten virgins calls people to be ready when the bridegroom arrives (Matt. 25:1–13). When he appears, he will usher those prepared and waiting for him "to the marriage feast" (Matt. 25:10). This parable, then, calls Jesus's disciples to be ready for his glorious return at the end of the age. Upon his return, he will gather them and bring them to a grand wedding banquet. In similar fashion and on the eve of his death, Jesus observes the faithfulness of his disciples to remain with him "in [his] trials" (Luke 22:28). He then tells them that the Father has given them the kingdom "that [they] may eat and drink at [his] table in [his] kingdom and sit on thrones judging the twelve tribes of Israel" (Luke 22:30). Once again, Jesus describes his kingdom in terms of his disciples' eating and drinking with him at a table that he has prepared for them.

What is striking is how wide-ranging the feast figure is in characterizing the kingdom. It captures the kingdom both in the future and in the present. It illustrates the kingdom as it goes to Jew and Gentile. It characterizes the fullness of the redemptive blessings that God gives to sinners in and through the Lord Jesus Christ. Describing the kingdom as a great banquet, furthermore, helps us to see how the kingdom is the fulfillment of what God promised his people of old under the Law and the Prophets.

Conclusion

From Genesis to Revelation, and at many points in between, God uses the image of a feast, meal, or banquet to characterize some of the most cherished teachings of Scripture. God prepares a bountiful table and invites the undeserving to sit with him there. The table, in all its abundance, points to the spiritual blessings that God gives his people—life, joy, peace, and glory. It points supremely to the chief blessing—God himself. The table represents God's condescension in drawing sinners to himself, redeeming them, and inviting them to communion with him. The glory of this communion is that it is not limited to this life. Death cannot rob us of it. In fact, Jesus stresses, the best is yet to come. We have been treated to an appetizer in this life. The fullness of the meal awaits us when the Savior returns.

There are, however, many threats and temptations that lie between us and that full meal. Jesus wants us to know that God is committed to bringing each and every one of his true children to that table. One of the ways that God expresses this commitment is through the Lord's Supper, a sign of the new covenant and the meal of the new covenant. In the next chapter we will consider the Lord's Supper and how God has designed it to bring blessing and help to his people in the wilderness sojourn of this life.

4

The Lord's Supper

We have seen that the Bible records a succession of covenants across human history. In the garden, God entered into a covenant with Adam and, in Adam, with all his ordinary offspring. Adam sinned against God and so broke that covenant, plunging himself and us into rebellion, curse, and death. But soon after the fall, God introduced a second covenant into history. This gracious covenant would administer to sinners the promises of salvation in Jesus Christ. The multiple covenants that God makes with sinners across redemptive history are really administrations of this one gracious covenant introduced to Adam and Eve in Genesis 3:15. As believers, we have the privilege and benefit of living under the climactic administration of this gracious covenant, the new covenant.

Along with covenants we have also observed that God provides "signs" to accompany these covenants. These signs serve to display tangibly the promises God has spoken to his people. The signs confirm to God's people the truth of his promises. In the hands of the Spirit, they strengthen faith, helping believers to combat unbelief and to serve God in this world.

One of the two covenant signs God institutes under the new covenant is the Lord's Supper. This particular sign is also a meal. We saw in the last chapter that meals are a recurring feature of God's dealings with his covenant people. The various meals in Scripture between God and human beings help us to see the abundant and gracious character of the blessings he provides us in union and communion with Jesus Christ. Specifically, these meals point in different ways to how God gives *himself* to his people.

With this framework in place, we are now poised to look at the meaning and significance of the Lord's Supper as a sign and meal of the new covenant. We will look first at what the Gospels have to say about the Lord's Supper. Then, after briefly looking at the testimony of Acts, we will see what the apostle Paul says about the Lord's Supper. We will close by thinking about the significance of the Supper for the life of the church today.

The Gospels

The Gospels according to Matthew, Mark, and Luke each record Jesus's institution of the Lord's Supper (Matt. 26:26–29; Mark 14:22–25; Luke 22:15–20).[1] The institution of the Lord's Supper takes place in the course of Jesus's and his disciples' observance of the Passover meal (see Matt. 26:17–20). Just prior to the institution of the Supper and during the Passover meal, Jesus predicts his betrayal by one of the twelve disciples (Matt. 26:21–25). This prediction brings into view the coming events of Jesus's arrest, trial, and crucifixion. When Jesus institutes the Lord's Supper, then, his suffering and death are at the forefront of his mind.

---

1. Although John documents the same meal (see John 13), he does not record the institution of the Lord's Supper. This omission is likely because John's Gospel appears to be designed to supplement Matthew, Mark, and Luke. That is, John did not record the institution of the Lord's Supper because he assumed that his readership was already familiar with it from Matthew, Mark, and Luke.

Each Gospel tells us that Jesus takes bread, blesses it, breaks it, and then distributes it to his disciples with a word of institution:

Take, eat; this is my body. (Matt. 26:26)

Take, this is my body. (Mark 14:22)

This is my body, which is given for you. Do this in remembrance of me. (Luke 22:19)

Each Gospel tells us that Jesus then takes a cup, gives thanks, and offers it to his disciples with an accompanying word of institution:[2]

Drink of it, all of you, for this is my blood of the covenant, which is poured out for many for the forgiveness of sins. (Matt. 26:27–28)

This is my blood of the covenant, which is poured out for many. (Mark 14:24)

This cup that is poured out for you is the new covenant in my blood. (Luke 22:20)

Matthew and Mark conclude Jesus's words about the bread and the cup with a promise:[3]

I tell you I will not drink again of this fruit of the vine until that day when I drink it new with you in my Father's kingdom. (Matt. 26:29)

---

2. Students of the Gospels have puzzled for centuries over Luke's inclusion of two cups (Luke 22:17–20), which frame the bread (Luke 22:19). Matthew, Mark, and Paul (1 Corinthians 11) simply record the bread followed by a single cup. One common resolution of this apparent discrepancy is that the Passover meal would have involved at least four cups, and Matthew, Mark, and Paul record one of these cups, while Luke records two of them.

3. Luke includes a similar statement ("For I tell you that from now on I will not drink of the fruit of the vine until the kingdom of God comes," Luke 22:18) but places it with Jesus's words surrounding the first cup.

> Truly, I say to you, I will not drink again of the fruit of the vine until that day when I drink it new in the kingdom of God. (Mark 14:25)

Following these words, Matthew and Mark tell us, Jesus and the disciples sing a hymn and go out to the Mount of Olives. Jesus then predicts the disciples' imminent abandonment of him (Matt. 26:30–35; Mark 14:26–31).[4]

We are now prepared to think about the significance of the Lord's Supper in the Synoptic Gospels' presentation of its institution. We will first look at the place of the Supper as a sign and meal within the unfolding covenants of redemptive history. Then we will be in a position to think about what the Supper signifies or communicates to God's new covenant people and how we are to observe it meaningfully.

The Lord's Supper in Redemptive History

The Gospels tell us that the Lord's Supper occupies a significant place within redemptive history. It looks back to events that precede it and looks forward to events that will follow it.

The Lord's Supper looks back to the Passover. Jesus institutes the Supper in the context of a Passover meal. The Supper is not annexed to the Passover meal, but it is part of the meal itself.[5] In light of this fact, what is striking is what we *do not* see in the Gospels' account of the institution of the Supper—a lamb. The lamb was the centerpiece of the Passover meal and, we presume, was part of the meal that Jesus and his disciples celebrated together on the eve of his death.

---

4. Luke records some of these events (Luke 22:39–46) but mentions additional words of Jesus in Luke 22:24–38 before he tells his readers that Jesus and the disciples left the upper room.

5. Scholars debate this point. For a helpful and concise argument why this Supper was a Passover meal, see Andreas Köstenberger, "Was the Last Supper a Passover Meal?," in *The Lord's Supper: Remembering and Proclaiming Christ until He Comes*, ed. Thomas R. Schreiner and Matthew R. Crawford, NAC Studies in Bible and Theology 10 (Nashville: B&H, 2010), 6–30.

The Gospels, however, make no mention of a lamb in connection with the Lord's Supper.

The reason that there is no lamb in the Lord's Supper is that Jesus Christ himself is the Passover Lamb of God (John 1:29, 36; 19:36; 1 Cor. 5:7). The yearly Passover lambs all pointed to and found their meaning in *the* Passover Lamb, Jesus Christ. He dies on the cross as the Passover Lamb of God. What the exodus Passover (and all subsequent Passover observances) anticipated now finds its fulfillment and realization in the death of Christ on Calvary. His shed blood will cover the sins of his people (Rom. 3:25). In Christ, God passes over his people in judgment, punishing their substitute for their sins (2 Cor. 5:21). As a result, every one who puts his or her trust in Christ has been redeemed "with the precious blood of Christ, like that of a lamb without blemish or spot" (1 Pet. 1:19).

There is a complementary way in which we see the Lord's Supper looking back to what has gone before it. The Passover meal was a founding ordinance of the old covenant. This meal was instituted on the eve of the Passover event and on the cusp of the exodus. The Passover and the exodus were the founding redemptive events of the covenant that God made with Israel through Moses at Mount Sinai.

In the Lord's Supper, Jesus announces that the "cup that is poured out for you is the *new covenant* in my blood" (Luke 22:20). The Supper, then, will be an ordinance of what Jesus calls the new covenant. This ordinance and the covenant to which it is joined point to the sacrificial death of Christ on the cross ("in my blood"). With the resurrection of Jesus, the death of Christ serves as the historical, redemptive foundation of the new covenant. Both covenants are founded upon a great redemptive event, and both covenants have a meal instituted to commemorate that event.

The new covenant is not something that first appears in the teaching of Jesus. As we saw in the first chapter, the prophet Jeremiah spoke of it centuries before (Jeremiah 31). In this promise of the new covenant, God pledged, among other things, to "forgive [sinners'] iniquity, and [he] will remember their sin no more" (31:34). God of course forgave the sins of his old covenant people before the new covenant era. Paul mentions Abraham and David as only two examples among many whose sins were forgiven before the ministry of Christ (see Rom. 4:1–25). God's promise in Jeremiah says that under the new covenant, the basis upon which God forgives his people in every age would once and for all be accomplished in history. Under the old covenant, God forgave his people because of the work of the Christ who was yet to come; under the new covenant, God forgives his people because of the work of Christ who has already come. For that reason, all the sacrifices, which served as so many shadows of Christ (Col. 2:16–17), came to their appointed end. The substance has come. There are no more Passover lambs because *the* Passover Lamb has come and accomplished his work of saving sinners in his death and resurrection.

Here we see an important difference between the Passover meal and the Lord's Supper. The Passover meal looked *forward* to the Messiah who had yet to come in history. The Lord's Supper looks *back* to the Messiah who has already come in history. We live not in the era of promise but in the era of fulfillment. We are the people of God upon whom "the end of the ages has come" (1 Cor. 10:11).

As important as it is to recognize that the Supper looks back to the finished redemptive work of Christ for sinners, it is no less important to realize that the Supper also looks *forward* into redemptive history. Jesus says, "I tell you I will not drink again of this fruit of the vine until that day when I drink it new with you in my Father's kingdom" (Matt. 26:29). Jesus tells his disciples that he will voluntarily refrain from drinking wine until a set time in the future. That time is linked to the "day" of "my Father's kingdom" or "the kingdom of God" (Mark 14:25; cf. Luke 22:18, "until the kingdom of God comes"). Jesus is thinking here of the kingdom of God in its consummate manifestation, when he returns in glory to judge the world, ushering his people into the full inheritance of the kingdom (Matt. 25:34), when they "will shine like the sun in the kingdom of their Father" (Matt. 13:43).

It is then that Jesus will resume drinking the fruit of the vine. He is anticipating, in other words, the great messianic banquet we saw in the last chapter to be the hope of the Prophets, which will be realized at the return of Christ (Matt. 25:10; Rev. 19:7). The Lord's Supper serves, then, to point the people of God in hope to the certain return of Christ and to the consummation of their salvation in Christ.

The Lord's Supper, therefore, always and simultaneously points in two directions, backward and forward. It points backward to the finished work of Christ on the cross. The Supper in particular underscores this finished work as the fulfillment of the words and works of God in redemptive history leading up to the cross. It also points forward to the certain hope of the glorious return of Christ at the end of the age. It reminds God's people of the certainty of this hope—that the great, promised messianic banquet awaits us. If God was faithful to bring his promised Son into the world the first time to live, die, and rise again for our salvation, we can surely trust his promise that Jesus will return at the end of the age to consummate the application of his saving work in our lives.

The Significance of the Lord's Supper

We have already begun to reflect on the Supper's significance by thinking about its place within redemptive history. We may now think more specifically about what, according to the Gospels, the Supper communicates to God's people when they observe it. To understand this point is to have a better grasp on how we may participate in the Supper more thoughtfully and purposefully.

The Supper has two basic elements or signs: bread and wine. Jesus establishes relationships between the bread and his body and between the cup and his blood. Each element is accompanied by particular actions. The bread is to be blessed, broken, distributed, and eaten. The cup is to be presented, distributed, and drunk. Luke tells us that the bread is to be received and eaten "in remembrance of me" (Luke 22:19). This command to remember applies to the cup as well (see 1 Cor. 11:25).

One matter to appreciate from these details of the Supper is that the elements that Christ has appointed to be distributed to his people are "blessed." The goal of this meal, then, is to bring blessing to Christ's people. We can better appreciate the significance of this blessing when we remember that, throughout God's covenants in history, "blessing" is the alternative to "curse." As we have seen in our study of the covenants, human beings in Adam are born into a state of sin and, therefore, are under a curse. Within the covenants that God makes with his people, God brings redemptive blessing. The reason that he can bless sinners who deserve curse is that his Son, who deserves blessing, voluntarily took upon himself on the cross the curse that they deserved (Gal. 3:13–14). The blessing that Jesus places on this meal cost him dearly—his own suffering and accursed death on the cross. For this reason, the Lord's Supper should be very special and precious to us.

We may understand how partakers of the Supper experience blessing by thinking further about the two signs in the Supper. In keeping with covenant signs generally, these signs are physical, tangible elements. The first is bread and the second is wine (in the cup). What is the significance of the bread and wine in the Supper? They represent Jesus's body and his blood, that is, they represent *him.* Jesus is offering himself to his people for their nourishment. What kind of nourishment does Jesus have in view? He has in mind the nourishment that the Savior provides his spiritually needy and sin-weary people. "All the salvation and redemption brought about by Christ for his disciples is founded in the body and blood he gives them to eat and drink at the Eucharist," says Herman Ridderbos.[6] This nourishment, of course, is a *spiritual* nourishment. Only through faith in Christ and, we will see later, by the ministry of the Holy Spirit does one benefit from what Jesus offers and provides in the Supper. That Jesus has in mind believing on him when he speaks of feeding upon him is evident from his teaching in John 6. In that discourse, he calls upon his hearers to eat his flesh and to drink his blood (John 6:53). Jesus is not commending cannibalism, but faith in him. After declaring, "I am the bread of life," he goes on to say, "whoever *comes to me* shall not hunger and whoever *believes in me* shall never thirst" (John 6:35). To feed on the body and to drink the blood of Christ, in the teaching of Jesus, is to come to Jesus and to believe upon him as the "living bread that came down from heaven" (John 6:51).

When we say, then, that the Lord's Supper is a memorial, we do not mean that it is a *bare* memorial. The Supper is an ordinance of remembrance—we are to eat the bread and drink the wine in remembrance of what Christ has done for us. But the meaning of the Supper is not the sum total of our unaided powers of reflection. To be sure, we must set our minds upon the spiritual realities presented before us in the Supper. But we engage our minds so that in the Supper we may commune with Jesus Christ by faith. The Supper is most profoundly an ordinance of communion with the Savior. Through

---

6. Herman Ridderbos, *The Coming of the Kingdom*, trans. H. de Jongste (Philadelphia: Presbyterian and Reformed, 1962), 417. "Eucharist" is a name that many in the history of the church have applied to the Lord's Supper. It comes from the Greek word meaning "thanksgiving" and describes the thankful remembrance that should characterize the Supper (1 Cor. 11:24–25).

faith, the believer meets with Christ who spiritually nourishes his or her soul in that meal.

What Jesus commands to be done with the bread and wine in the Lord's Supper helps us to understand more of the Supper's meaning. The bread is broken and given; the cup is presented and distributed. Specifically, the cup represents "[the] blood of the covenant, which is poured out for many for the forgiveness of sins" (Matt. 26:28). Soon after he utters these words and distributes the bread and the wine in the upper room, Christ gives his body and pours out his own blood on the cross. In the Lord's Supper, Jesus gives himself to his people as their Redeemer, as the one who at the cross has laid down his life as an offering for their sins and, along with his resurrection, has secured for them glory, blessing, and life. Every time we witness the breaking and giving of the bread and the presentation and distribution of the cup in the Lord's Supper, we are reminded of Jesus's selfless self-giving for our salvation. Jesus is our life and nourishment because he gave himself for us on the cross.

That Christ appointed the elements of bread and wine to be distributed to us powerfully portrays one of the most basic lessons in Jesus's teaching about salvation. That lesson is that we are undeserving recipients of the free provision of God in Christ. The Lord's Supper is of a piece with Jesus's teaching about the kingdom of God (Matt. 26:29 and parallels). The Supper symbolically reinforces a lesson that Jesus taught frequently about the kingdom—it is the gift of God to human beings whom Jesus characterizes as "poor," that is, helpless and in need of salvation (Luke 22:29; 4:18). This gift of the kingdom to people is the "good pleasure" of the Father (Luke 12:32; cf. 10:21–22). The Father does not give the gift of the kingdom to those who deserve it or show promise. He gives it solely according to the counsel of his will. This gift, furthermore, is available only in Christ, to whom "all things have been handed" by the Father (Luke

10:22). In the Lord's Supper, Jesus comes to us and meets us at our point of need. He does not wait for us to come to him. We *do* come to him in faith—a faith that is the grace-provided response to his overtures of mercy and his pledge of spiritual presence to us. When we come to Christ in the Supper, we are not fundamentally doing something for him. He is, rather, doing something for us. He is supplying needy souls with the grace of the gospel. He is furnishing what we need from the resources of his sacrificial death on the cross. He is pledging to bring each of his children home to the messianic banquet where we shall enjoy in full what we now enjoy in part—life and blessing from, with, and in our Savior.

We have, to this point, been thinking about the Lord's Supper's significance in terms of the relation of the individual believer to Christ in that meal. However, our understanding of the Supper from the Gospels would be incomplete if we failed to see an additional dimension to this meal—in the Supper, we are gathering together as the family of God to commune with our Savior.

Recall that Christ chose to institute the Supper in the course of the Passover meal. The Passover meal was a family ordinance. God appointed families to gather together and to feed upon the sacrificed lamb. The father, in particular, had the responsibility of explaining to his sons the spiritual significance of the Passover (see Ex. 12:26–27; cf. 13:8, 14). When Christ gathers together the disciples for a Passover meal, he is testifying to the character of the new covenant people of God as a family (cf. Matt. 23:8–10; Mark 3:31–35). The Lord's Supper, therefore, is the corresponding family meal under the new covenant. Jesus's disciples partake of the Supper under the oversight and tutelage of their heavenly Father and elder Brother. The Lord's Supper carries with it responsibilities, privileges, and benefits that fall to individuals, but it is not an individualistic meal. It is a family meal. By Jesus's appointment, every time the Lord's Supper is observed, the people of God are reminded of their identity as the family of God, supernaturally created and sustained by the grace of God.

By implication, the fact that the Supper is a family meal reinforces a distinction between the church and those who are not part of the church. That is, Jesus does not invite all humanity to his Table. He invites his disciples to come. When we partake of the Lord's Supper, we are declaring to one another and to the world around us that we are no longer part of the world. By the grace of Christ, we have been brought out of the world and into the family of God.

The Gospels tell us, then, that the Lord's Supper has three interwoven dimensions. First, it is a covenant meal in which individual believers, by faith, commune with Christ to their spiritual nourishment. This meal is designed not to create faith anew but to strengthen the existing faith of Christ's disciples. Second, it is a family meal in which the covenant family of God gathers together under the oversight of God in Christ. The Supper should serve, then, to promote the familial bonds that exist within the people of God. Third, the Lord's Supper serves to distinguish the church as a society that God has set apart from the world around them. This declaration is not one of smug pride or self-righteousness. On the contrary, it is the church testifying to the saving grace of God, which draws sinners from their sin to the Lord Jesus Christ for salvation. Although outsiders are not invited to the Table, the visible display of the death of Christ in the Supper is a powerful representation of the gospel of Christ for sinners. The Supper is thus a standing evangelistic invitation to unbelievers—not to come to the Table, but to come to Jesus Christ in faith for the covering of their sins by the blood of the true Passover Lamb of God. If and when they come to Christ by faith, they may later come to the Table as members of the family who have a share in that Table.

Acts

Now that we have looked at the Gospels, we may consider the testimony of Acts and, later, Paul. While Acts does not offer a lot of information about the Lord's Supper, the information it does provide is important to our understanding of the Supper and its practice in the church soon after the resurrection of Christ. We may look at two passages in particular.

The first is Acts 2:42, "And they devoted themselves to the apostles' teaching and the fellowship, to the breaking of bread and the prayers." This statement follows Peter's sermon on the day of Pentecost and the remarkable conversion to Christ of "about three thousand souls," who were added to the number of the church (Acts 2:41). In Luke's description of the early church, he points to four activities that characterized its life: "devot[ion] to the apostles' teaching," "fellowship," "the breaking of bread," and "the prayers" (Acts 2:42). Although some have argued that "the breaking of bread" simply refers to everyday meals among Christians, it more likely refers to the observance of the Lord's Supper.[7] Significantly, Luke's reference to the Lord's Supper follows two matters that the Synoptics regard as crucial to the proper observance of the Supper. The first is "the apostles' teaching." The Acts of the Apostles tell us that the apostles were Christ's appointed witnesses to him (Acts 1:8). They were the beneficiary of forty days of the risen Jesus's teaching about the kingdom of God (Acts 1:3). Acts shows that the apostles' teaching found its focal point in the death and resurrection of Christ, according to the Scripture, for the salvation of sinners. The Lord's Supper is a covenant sign, a visible representation of the cross of Christ for the remembrance

---

7. Compare the nearly identical phrase in Acts 20:7, where there is no question that the Lord's Supper is being observed. Furthermore, the fact that the word "bread" in Acts 2:42 carries the definite article in the Greek text suggests that what Luke is describing rises above an ordinary meal.

and profit of the church. The Supper has meaning and significance in light of the apostles' teaching in the New Testament. Just as the early church devoted itself to the apostolic Word of God, so also it devoted itself to the accompanying new covenant sign of the Lord's Supper. The second is "fellowship." We have seen how the Synoptic Gospels point to the Supper as a meal of the new covenant community. Just as the Supper is a means of believers' communion with Christ, so also it brings to visible expression the communion of believers with one another. The church's devotion to the Lord's Supper is entirely understandable in light of its prioritization of fellowship.

The second passage is Acts 20:7, 11:

> On the first day of the week, when we were gathered together to break bread, Paul talked with [the church in Troas], intending to depart on the next day, and he prolonged his speech until midnight. . . . And when Paul had gone up and had broken bread and eaten, he conversed with them a long while, until daybreak, and so departed.

In this passage, Luke gives us a description of how the early church observed the Lord's Supper, to which they were devoted. First, it was a communal observance. The church gathered together in order to enjoy this meal. We do not read of unbelievers or outsiders joining the meal. It was and is only for the covenant community. Second, it was an act of worship. The breaking of bread took place "on the first day of the week," which the early church, under the leadership of the apostles, recognized and set apart as the day of worship that Christ had appointed for his new covenant people (see also 1 Cor. 16:2; Rev. 1:10). As such, the Lord's Supper would have been a regular, even frequent, element of the church's gathered worship. Third, it accompanied the preaching of the Word. Paul preceded and followed the

Lord's Supper with public proclamation. In keeping with the pattern of covenant signs generally, covenant words frame and interpret this covenant sign. The gospel verbally proclaimed provides necessary context for the gospel displayed to all the senses.

Acts shows us, then, that the church was faithful to keep Jesus's command to observe the Lord's Supper in remembrance of him. It appears to have been a standing or recurring feature of the church's worship, just as Jesus had called the church to observe the Supper until he returns. It serves simultaneously as both sign and meal of the new covenant. For this covenant meal, the people of God assemble and feed together.

The one who presided over the administration of the Supper in Troas was the apostle Paul. If we want to know what Paul understood the Supper to mean and its significance in the life of the church, we need only turn to his letters. It is in 1 Corinthians that Paul helps us understand the Lord's Supper with clarity and depth.

Paul

Before I take up what Paul has to say about the Lord's Supper in 1 Corinthians, it is important to place his statements in the context of the whole letter. Paul served the church in Corinth for at least a year and a half (Acts 18:11). He therefore had a close and intimate relationship with that church. His correspondence with the church reflects a relationship that was also occasionally turbulent. In 1 Corinthians, Paul must address a host of issues, some of which have been brought to his attention by concerned parties in the church (1 Cor. 1:11; 5:1), others of which have been directed to him by official correspondence from the church (1 Cor. 7:1; 8:1). Paul devotes considerable space to the problem of divisions within the church (1 Cor. 1:10–4:21). Members have sinfully divided into factions organized around prominent leaders within the church. Paul (presumably speaking for the other leaders as well) categorically disavows such divisions. The way in which he will promote unity is by applying the gospel to the situation in Corinth (1 Cor. 1:18; 2:1–5). This gospel promotes true unity and dissolves any spirit that leads to division and faction in the church.

Another set of issues that Paul must address concerns the church's failure to define itself properly, in both thought and life, with respect to the world. This failure has manifested itself in profound confusion regarding sexual morality (see 1 Corinthians 5–7). It has also displayed itself in the church members' participation in idolatrous meals (see 1 Corinthians 8–10). Paul has to admonish the Corinthians for eating food "in an idol's temple" (1 Cor. 8:10) and to counsel them concerning whether or when they might eat food that has been offered to an idol (1 Cor. 10:23–11:1). The apostle detects an unreflective permissiveness within the church that runs counter to their profession of the lordship of Christ.

These two issues—divisions in the church and compromise with the world—frame Paul's teaching about the Lord's Supper in 1 Corinthians. Paul addresses the Supper in two passages in this letter. The first is 1 Corinthians 10:14–22, which follows a grim account of Israel's unfaithfulness in the wilderness and begins with the command "Flee from idolatry" (10:14). Paul here offers specific counsel regarding eating meals with unbelievers. The second is 1 Corinthians 11:17–34, where Paul addresses the observance of the Lord's Supper and how it has been marred by factionalism and exclusion within the church (11:18–19). The way the Corinthians are observing the Supper reflects the disorder characterizing the church's public worship generally (see 1 Cor. 11:2–16; 14:26–40). Matters have become so bad that Paul informs the church, "When you come together it is not for the better but for the worse," and "When you come together, it is not the Lord's Supper that you eat" (1 Cor. 11:17, 20). Paul's teaching about the Lord's Supper, then, is woven into his broader pastoral response to the problems facing the church in Corinth.

How then does Paul explain the meaning and significance of the Supper to the troubled Corinthian church? He not only reinforces what the Supper is but also gives the church guidance regarding its proper observance. In doing so, he stresses that his teaching about the Supper has come directly and without modification from the Lord Jesus Christ: "For I received from the Lord what I also delivered to you" (1 Cor. 11:23). What follows resembles the Gospels' account (especially Luke's) of the institution of the Lord's Supper.

> The Lord Jesus on the night when he was betrayed took bread, and when he had given thanks, he broke it, and said, "This is my body, which is for you. Do this in remembrance of me." In the same way also he took the cup, after supper, saying, "This cup is the new covenant in my blood. Do this, as often as you drink it, in remembrance of me." For as often as you eat this bread and drink the cup, you proclaim the Lord's death until he comes. (1 Cor. 11:23b–26)

Here Paul restates Jesus's own teaching about the Lord's Supper. The Supper is an ordinance that belongs to the "new covenant" that Christ establishes in his "blood," that is, in his death on the cross. It is, therefore, a covenant meal whose focus is remembrance of the great work of God in Christ to redeem sinners from their sins. Specifically, the Supper looks back to the cross, namely, the once-for-all sacrifice of Christ for his people. The Supper also looks forward—believers "proclaim the Lord's death until he comes." The Supper articulates not only the reality of Christ's atoning, substitutionary death for sinners but also the certainty of his future and glorious return.

Paul's account of the Supper confirms much of what we have

learned already. There are two basic elements or signs: bread and wine. The bread is blessed, broken, distributed, and eaten. The cup is set apart, distributed, and drunk. The bread and wine stand for the body and blood of Christ, respectively. Christ gives them "for" his disciples. When he does so, Christ is offering himself to his people. The price of this blessed self-giving is his own death on the cross ("blood," "Lord's death"). The Supper is, moreover, an enacted remembrance of Christ, particularly his death on the cross. As we shall see, for Paul this remembrance is not that of a bare memorial. It is an occasion when Christ meets with his disciples to give himself in blessing. He does this as they exercise faith in him.

If there is a vertical dimension to the Supper, there is also a horizontal dimension to the Supper. Because of the pastoral problems in Corinth, this latter dimension receives most of Paul's attention. One should not conclude, however, that this horizontal dimension is of primary importance to Paul, as though the Supper were exclusively or mainly a community meal. It *is* a community meal but only as it is first a meal of communion between Christ and believers. Paul, in fact, helps the church understand the horizontal significance of the Supper precisely by setting that aspect within the larger context of the Supper's vertical significance. This point is evident in both of the 1 Corinthians passages in which Paul addresses the Lord's Supper.

1 Corinthians 10:14–22

In 1 Corinthians 11:23–26, Paul will remind the church that the Supper is an ordinance of remembrance. The Supper commemorates the death of Christ for sinners and his self-giving in blessing to his people. But this meal is at the same time an ordinance of communion between the believer and Christ. Paul stresses this point in 1 Corinthians 10:14–22. In verse 16, he tells the church, "The cup of blessing that we bless, is it not a participation in the blood of Christ? The bread that we break, is it not a participation in the body of Christ?" The language that Paul uses is language he will use of the Supper in the next chapter (see 1 Cor. 11:23–26). He is therefore speaking of the Lord's Supper in 1 Corinthians 10:14–22.

In these verses, the apostle introduces the word "participation" (Greek, *koinōnia*). Paul uses forms of this word in his instruction that follows. The Israelites "who eat the sacrifices [are] participants [*koinōnoi*] in the altar" (1 Cor. 10:18). Paul then warns the Corinthians against participating in pagan idolatry: "What pagans sacrifice they offer to demons and not to God. I do not want you to be participants [*koinōnous*] with demons. You cannot drink the cup of the Lord and the cup of demons. You cannot partake of the table of the Lord and the table of demons" (1 Cor. 10:20–21). Believers who take the Lord's Supper enter into communion with Christ—they participate in his body and blood. For this reason, it is utterly improper for them also to partake of food that they know has been offered to idols. Partaking of such food entails communion with demons. Christ's lordship is exclusive—believers may not partake of the Lord's Table and a demon's table.

Paul says that believers, in the Supper, commune in the body and blood of Christ. In other words, believers commune with Christ himself and in this way have access to all the benefits he won for them in his life, death, and resurrection. To understand how believers commune with Christ in the Supper, we may reflect on how believers commune with Christ generally. According to Paul's teaching elsewhere, believers commune with Christ *by the Spirit who works by and with the Word* and *through faith.* It is the Spirit who is the bond of our union with Christ and who applies to us over time what Christ accomplished for us in his death and resurrection (see Rom. 8:1–17; Eph. 3:16–17). In this way, the Spirit brings us into communion with Christ. From our human vantage point, it is by the exercise of faith that we enter into communion with Christ (see Gal. 2:20). The Supper is an especially rich occasion for believers to commune with Christ. He meets with his people by the ministry of his Spirit; at one and the same time, we meet with Christ in the exercise of faith. In the Supper, Christ is spiritually present to believers through faith in Christ.

This profound expression of communion with Christ in the Supper has equally profound horizontal implications. "Because there is one bread, we who are many are one body, for we all partake of the one bread" (1 Cor. 10:17). Whereas "body" in the previous verse refers to Christ offered to his people in the Supper, "body" here refers to the church, the people of God, the body of Christ. For Paul, "the unity of the church . . . is denoted in virtue of its common share in the one bread and therein in the sacrifice made for it by Christ," Ridderbos explains.[8] The work of Christ, represented in the Supper, defines the unity of the church. The church is one insofar as its members share in the one sacrifice of Christ for sinners, Jew and Gentile (cf. Rom. 3:21–31). For this reason, worldly divisions and the exclusion of those whom the world deems inferior have no place in the church (cf. Eph. 4:3–6). The vertical character of the Lord's Supper has palpable and necessary implications for the horizontal character of its observance in the church.

1 CORINTHIANS 11:17–34

In 1 Corinthians 11:17–34, Paul returns to the matter of the observance of the Lord's Supper in the church in Corinth. We have seen how, in verses 23–26, Paul reiterates and amplifies the teaching of Jesus concerning the Supper, as that teaching has been "received" by Paul and so "delivered" to the church (11:23). Framing this paragraph of instruction are two passages that address the Corinthians' abuses of the Lord's Supper (11:17–22, 27–34).

In 1 Corinthians 11:17–22, Paul identifies the church's sins and

---

8. Herman N. Ridderbos, *Paul: An Outline of His Theology*, trans. J. R. DeWitt (Grand Rapids, MI: Eerdmans, 1975), 375.

admonishes the Corinthians for them. The "divisions" and "factions" present in the church lamentably manifest themselves when the church gathers, that is, for the Lord's Supper (11:18–19). This problem is so serious, we have seen, that Paul is unwilling to call what transpires there the Lord's Supper (11:20). What is symptomatic of this division in the Corinthians' observance of the Supper? It is "every man for himself," privileged individuals selfishly consuming food and drink, even to the point of intoxication, while their Christian brothers of more modest means look on in hunger (1 Cor. 11:21). This practice "despise[s] the church of God and humiliate[s] those who have nothing" (11:22).

It is at this point that Paul restates the apostolic doctrine of the Lord's Supper (1 Cor. 11:23–26). As in the previous chapter, Paul appeals to the vertical character of the Supper in order to correct problems transpiring at the horizontal level. Before he issues particular commands to remedy the problem in Corinth, the church must first understand the Supper's meaning in relation to Christ. Paul's closing statement brings this portion of his argument to a close and prepares the way for his prescriptions in 1 Corinthians 11:27–34: "For as often as you eat and drink the cup, you proclaim the Lord's death until he comes" (11:26). The Supper should be a united church's proclamation of the death of Christ. The church's horizontal abuses have struck at the very heart of the meaning of the Supper, an ordinance that publicly and visibly sets forth the gospel of Christ.

In the remaining verses, Paul delivers commands and warnings to the church in its observance of the Supper (1 Cor. 11:27–34). The commands in 1 Corinthians 11:27–29 are of general or broad application; those in verses 30–34 specifically relate to the church in Corinth. A person must perform two duties before eating the bread or drinking the cup: "let a person examine himself" (11:28); one must "discer[n] the body" (11:29). What should the focus of self-examination be, and how should a person discern the body? In light of what Paul teaches in 1 Corinthians 11:23–26, a person must examine himself whether he understands the meaning and significance of the Lord's Supper; whether he is prepared, in faith, to commune with the Lord Jesus Christ; whether his conduct is consistent with that of a professed follower of Christ. To discern the body is to understand in what sense the bread is the body of Christ. With such an understanding, a person will not approach the Lord's Table casually or cavalierly. He or she will approach it with all the reverence due a covenant meal.

Even as there is blessing to be found in communing with Christ, by the Spirit and through faith, so there are consequences for careless attendance at the Table. To eat and drink "in an unworthy manner" renders one "guilty" of profaning "the body and blood of the Lord" (1 Cor. 11:27). If one "eats and drinks without discerning the body," he "eats and drinks judgment on himself" (1 Cor. 11:29). For this reason, Paul points out, "many of you are weak and ill, and some have died" (1 Cor. 11:30). The apostle explains in the following verses that these consequences represent the Lord's chastening discipline of his people, not the kind of condemnation under which the world lies (1 Cor. 11:32). God's goal in this chastening discipline is that the erring party would repent and commit himself to obeying Christ (see 1 Cor. 11:33–34). If a person, however, persists in his sin and refuses to repent, he eventually evidences that he is truly part of the world. Nothing remains for him but condemnation or covenant curse.

Because the Lord's Supper is a sign and meal of the new covenant, it carries with it the potential for both blessing and curse. Blessing and curse are not, of course, automatically dispensed. They indicate, rather, the ways in which Christ responds to those who approach his Table.[9] He reserves blessing for those who, examining themselves

---

9. "Blessing and curse are not automatically given with the elements, nor are both joined to them in an equally essential way, but it is the living Lord himself who . . . deals with the church according to his gracious and righteous redemptive will" (Ridderbos, *Paul*, 427, cited by George W. Knight, "1 Corinthians 11:17–34: The Lord's Supper: Abuses, Words of Institution

and discerning the body, commune with Christ in faith through the Supper and exhibit genuine communion and unity with their fellow believers. Those within the covenant community who fail here are subject to the Lord's covenantal discipline designed to bring them to repentance. Those, however, who persist in abusing and profaning this covenant ordinance have nothing to anticipate but covenant curse. Because the bread and wine are not *bare* signs and *bare* memorials, but function in the context of the new covenant, it matters a great deal how one conducts himself in the Lord's Supper.

SUMMARIZING PAUL'S VIEW

In summary, the Lord's Supper operates, for Paul, along at least three lines.

First, it is the occasion of the covenant member's communion with the covenant Head, Jesus Christ. In the Lord's Supper, Christ is present to his people by the Holy Spirit and through faith (1 Cor. 10:16). The believer, examining himself, discerning the body and blood of the Lord and so, communing with Christ by faith, finds himself spiritually nourished by what Christ is pleased to provide in the Supper. Christ is pleased to provide himself and all the benefits he has won for his people. What the Supper particularly brings to the fore is the death of Christ for sinners. Believers seek and find blessing from the One who underwent covenant curse on their behalf.

In the second place, the Lord's Supper is a demonstration of the unity of the church. One reason why the unity of the church is so important to Paul in this context is that the observance of the Supper "proclaim[s] the Lord's death until he comes" (1 Cor. 11:26). This proclamation is a *corporate* proclamation. The covenant community

---

and Warnings and the Inferences and Deductions with Respect to Paedocommunion," in Guy Waters and Ligon Duncan, *Children and the Lord's Supper: Let a Man Examine Himself* (Fearn, Ross-shire, Scotland: Christian Focus, 2011), 92n33.

stands as one redeemed people before their Savior and declares to the world that Christ gave his life in order to redeem all kinds of people, even the weak and despised in the world. For Paul, this horizontal dimension of the Supper is not negotiable or dispensable. The egregious breaches of church unity in Corinth had so corrupted the Supper that it ceased any longer to be the Supper (1 Cor. 11:20).

Third and finally, the Lord's Supper draws a clear line between the church and the world. Significantly, the church in Corinth had often failed to maintain this clear distinction. In light of this failure, Paul emphasized the fact that, in the Supper, we not only commune with Christ but also renounce communing with idols or demons. Communion with Christ requires believers to make a decided break with anything that would compete with or challenge the exclusive prerogatives of the lordship of Christ. Although the church is not called to leave the world (1 Cor. 5:10), its members are called to be different from the world. The Lord's Supper serves to distinguish the church from outsiders. As with other covenant signs and covenant meals, the Supper covenantally delineates the sphere of blessing from the sphere of curse. Simply being a member of the covenant community is no guarantee, of course, of receiving covenant blessing from Christ. But outside this sphere, there is no hope of blessing.

Conclusion

The Lord's Supper is a sign and a meal that Christ appointed for the new covenant community. As such, it stands in line with the signs and meals that God has appointed within his covenants across redemptive history. It furthermore points us forward to the consummation of our redemption at the great messianic banquet, when the tree of life will be made available to us. In the next chapter, we will conclude our study by summarizing our findings and thinking further about the nature and importance of the Supper for the life of God's people today.

5

Conclusions for the Church

As we bring this biblical-theological study of the Lord's Supper to a close, it may be helpful to review in brief what we have seen the Scripture to teach. I will then address a few questions that often arise in the church concerning the Lord's Supper.

A Review of the Biblical Teaching

From Genesis to Revelation, there is a succession of covenants. There are basically two covenants in the Bible: the covenant of works and the covenant of grace. God made the covenant of works in the garden with Adam and, in Adam, with all his ordinary descendants. This covenant was conditioned upon Adam's obedience. When our representative Adam disobeyed God, he plunged himself and all of us into sin and misery. The way to eschatological or eternal life by our obedience was forever closed off.

Soon after Adam's fall into sin, God introduced a second covenant into history, the covenant of grace. This covenant was conditioned upon the obedience of the second and last Adam, Jesus Christ. He pledged to obey where we failed to obey. Part of his obedience involved bearing the penalty due to us for our sin. On the basis of his obedience, those who trust in him are brought from covenant curse to covenant blessing. God instituted this covenant in history in Genesis 3:15. By a series of covenantal administrations, progressively revealed in redemptive history, God expanded and extended the gospel promises that the covenant of grace administers to sinners.[1] Whatever differences there are among these administrations (and there are differences), underlying those differences is a fundamental unity—the salvation of sinners in and by the work of Jesus Christ.

As a help to the faith of his people, God has appointed signs within his covenants with human beings. These signs are a standing feature of the various administrations of the covenant of grace. Having the sign is no guarantee or assurance of salvation. Nor does having the sign mean that one has faith. But it is a great blessing to have the sign insofar as it directs us to the promise signified and confirms to us the truth of God's promise.

The Bible begins and ends with the tree of life. The tree of life first functioned as a covenantal sign or pledge in the covenant of works. It represents to new covenant believers the consummation of our salvation. Significantly, the tree of life is something that people eat or consume. We noted that, throughout redemptive history, God has appointed covenant meals for his people. While these meals are necessarily physical and tangible, they point beyond themselves to the spiritual realities that God pledges to his people in covenant with him. Specifically, they point to the greatest blessing of all—God himself in communion with his people. The Prophets, in particular, direct the people of God to a great banquet or feast in which God abundantly provides for all the spiritual needs of his people. The New

---

1. We reviewed these administrations in an earlier chapter. They are the Adamic (after the fall), Noahic, Abrahamic, Mosaic, Davidic, and new covenants. Each is a covenantal administration of the one covenant of grace.

Testament tells us that Christ has come to do just that. What the Law and the Prophets pointed to and anticipated in these feasts, Christ in his life, death, and resurrection has accomplished. God's new covenant people have begun to enjoy life and blessing in Christ, but the fullness of these awaits his return at the end of the age.

As we await that fullness, we enjoy the new covenant meal that Christ has set for us, the Lord's Supper. The Supper is both sign *and* meal. It displaces the old covenant Passover feast. What Passover anticipated, the Lord's Supper declares as accomplished. The realities to which Passover looked *forward* are the realities to which the Lord's Supper looks *back*.

The Supper invites us to remember the Lord Jesus Christ, on whose body we feed and whose blood we drink, through faith in him. The Lord's Supper represents to the senses of God's people the death of Christ for sinners. It reinforces one of the most basic lessons of Jesus's teaching, that salvation is by the grace of God alone for the undeserving. In the Supper, Christ invites his needy people to come to him to be filled with spiritual nourishment. This happens when, in this meal, God's people commune with their living Savior by faith, in the power of the Spirit, who works by and with the Word of Christ. For these reasons, the Supper is not fundamentally something we do for Christ. It represents, in the first instance, what Christ has done for us.

The ongoing repetition of the Lord's Supper in the life of the church and our continuing need for the grace that Christ supplies to faith in the Supper underscores another basic message of this meal. The Lord's Supper not only points us back to Christ's first appearing but also points us forward to Christ's second appearing, his glorious return at the end of the age. When Christ returns, he will gather his people and bring them to the eschatological banquet that he has prepared for them. The Lord's Supper anticipates that glorious feast. In this way, the new covenant meal stirs our hope for Christ's return.

The Lord's Supper carries with it important social or horizontal dimensions. The Supper is a powerful display of the unity of God's people and their identity as the family of God and the covenant community. The Supper, in this fashion, distinguishes the church from the world. It confirms to God's people their commitment to the exclusive claims of the lordship of Christ and calls them to separate from ungodly participation in the world around them. For these reasons, worldly disunity and other ungodly behavior palpably affect the church's experience of the Lord's Supper. Paul, in particular, points to a necessary subjective preparation for the Lord's Supper—we must examine ourselves and discern the body and blood of Christ. In a severe mercy, God is prepared to chasten his people who profane and otherwise misuse the Supper. Those who persist in so doing will find nothing but curse waiting for them. As a covenant sign, the Supper is, in Christ's hands, an occasion of blessing and curse. Paul instructs and urges the church to ensure that it is an occasion of blessing.

Three Questions in the Life of the Church

We may now take up three questions that Christians have asked about the Supper and address them in light of our biblical-theological study. How is Christ present in the Supper? Who may come to the Supper? How is the Supper like and unlike baptism?

How Is Christ Present in the Supper?

We have seen the New Testament writers stress that Christ is present at the Supper he has appointed for his people. This is a running characteristic of covenant meals—the presence of God with his people for their blessing. Any understanding of the Supper that reduces it to a bare memorial or a mere exercise of intellectual recollection of the meaning of the cross is inadequate. Of course, the Supper is an ordinance of remembrance, and recipients must turn their minds to the cross as they approach the Table. But when they come to the Table, they expect to meet their Savior.

How, then, is Christ present to them? Throughout the centuries, many in the church have identified Christ's presence with the elements of bread and wine. That is, Christ is thought to be corporally or physically present in, with, or under the bread and wine. But these views suffer from grave problems. To name just one, to identify the humanity of Christ with the bread and wine destroys the very character of the Supper as a covenant *sign*. By definition, a covenant sign points beyond itself to certain spiritual realities. The bread and wine must not be physically identified with Jesus Christ, since Christ appointed the bread and wine to point toward him as the Savior of his people. We may observe, furthermore, that it is not the bread and wine of themselves that point to Jesus Christ. It is the *bread given and received* and the *cup distributed and received* that point to Jesus Christ.[2]

Christ *is* present in the Supper, but he is present to his people in the Supper in the way that he is present to his people on any other occasion, by the ministry of the Holy Spirit working by and with the Word of God, to the faith of the believer. We may affirm, then, that the bread and wine are the body and blood of Christ not physically or superstitiously but spiritually for God's people, as we approach the Table and feed upon Christ by faith. At this covenant meal, we truly dine with our covenant Head.

---

2. "The Roman Catholic and the old Lutheran exegesis do not err because of the close connection they established between bread and body, wine and blood, but in that they made the symbol itself into the reality whereas they should have realized that the connection between the symbol and its intended reality is to be sought in the action of giving, on the one hand, and in that of eating and drinking, on the other" (Herman Ridderbos, *The Coming of the Kingdom*, trans. H. de Jongste [Philadelphia: Presbyterian and Reformed, 1962], 435).

Who May Come to the Supper?

It seems obvious that believers may come to the Lord's Supper. But because of the warnings that Paul issues in 1 Corinthians 11:27–34, we need a more nuanced understanding of who may come. We may make three further observations.

First, the Supper is available to those believers who have demonstrated the capacity to examine themselves and to discern the body and blood of Christ. They must understand the gospel. They must have an awareness and sense of their own sin. They must be trusting in Christ for their salvation and endeavoring to walk in obedience before him. They must be carrying out their pledged obligations of fellowship and unity with the local church, the body of Christ.

To be sure, every individual must decide for himself if he meets these qualifications. But because the Supper is a covenant meal, entrusted to the covenant community and administered by Christ's ministers, it is left to the elders to admit or exclude individuals from this Table. In many churches, once a person makes a believable declaration of faith in Jesus Christ, the elders gladly admit that person to the Lord's Table. Ultimately, however, as Paul reminds us, responsibility lies with the individual for communing properly (1 Cor. 11:27).

Second, there are occasions when even professing Christians should be barred from the Table by the elders. Paul envisions such a situation in 1 Corinthians 5. He tells the church "not to associate with anyone who bears the name of brother if he is guilty of sexual immorality or greed, or is an idolater, reviler, drunkard, or swindler—*not even to eat with such a one*" (5:11). Paul has in mind a person who is a professing Christian and is known for a lifestyle of sin. He forbids the church from eating with such a person. Whatever else the prohibition of eating with such a person may mean, Paul certainly has in mind the Lord's Supper. It is incongruous for an impenitent sinner to approach a Table representing the death of Christ for sin. It is wrong for one who knowingly and willingly gives himself to a particular sin to seek to commune in this ordinance with the Lord Jesus Christ.

Paul is not necessarily saying that this person is unsaved. The offender may well be a Christian. His exclusion from the Table is not designed to punish him. It is designed to chasten him and to recover him to full communion with Christ and his people. How is that the case? By being excluded from the "cup of blessing," wayward individuals should be reminded of the curse to which they are subject for sin, apart from the grace of Christ (1 Cor. 10:16). They should see that unless they repent and turn from their sin to Jesus Christ, they will perish eternally, under the covenant curse of Christ. This realization should prompt them to repentance and faith and, upon restoration, to return to the Table.

It is also necessary to exclude offenders from the Table for another reason. When professing Christians have a reputation for particular sins, they threaten the holiness and integrity of the church (1 Cor. 5:7). In the eyes of onlookers, at least, they blur the line between the church and the world, between the covenant community and the realm of curse. For the purity and reputation of the church, they should be prevented from approaching the Table and partaking of the bread and wine.

Third, there are times when professing Christians, because of doubts, a strong sense of sin, weak faith, or a host of other reasons, may hesitate to come to the Table. Certainly Christians in these situations should seek trusted Christian counsel and not struggle on their own. One of the things that they should realize is that Christ appointed the Table not for the deserving but for the undeserving.[3] The Table is

---

3. When Paul says that we should not partake "in an unworthy manner" (1 Cor. 11:27), he is not saying that we need to be worthy people before we may take the Lord's Supper. He is speaking, rather, of the way in which Christians are or are not to approach the Table.

for sinners who know that they are sinners, who have put their trust in Christ and sincerely desire to serve him, and who are recognized members of the family of God. The Table is not a reward for good behavior. It is a helping hand for believers struggling with doubts, unbelief, and other sins. Exiling oneself from the Table may be the very worst thing spiritually for a struggling Christian. The Table is designed to provide, by the Spirit working through and with the Word, the very thing the struggling individual desperately needs—strengthened faith.

How Is the Lord's Supper Like and Unlike Baptism?

Finally, we may ask how the Lord's Supper compares with the other covenant sign that Christ has appointed for the new covenant community, baptism. Baptism and the Lord's Supper are alike in a number of ways. Christ has instituted both. Each is an ordinance unique to the new covenant. Each is to be observed only within the new covenant community. Each serves to point the recipient to Christ and the benefits of his salvation. Each is to be observed until Christ returns at the end of the age.

But Baptism and the Lord's Supper differ in important ways as well, even beyond the obvious difference that baptism is to be administered with water, and the Lord's Supper with bread and wine. Baptism and the Lord's Supper have different old covenant analogs. The sign and seal of circumcision corresponds to baptism (Col. 2:11–12); the sign and seal of Passover corresponds to the Lord's Supper. Moreover, baptism and the Lord's Supper have different signification. While each points to Christ, each does so distinctly. Baptism points particularly to our union with Christ, especially in his death and resurrection (see Rom. 6:1–23; Gal. 3:27). The Lord's Supper points particularly to the cross of Christ, the redemptive and sacrificial death of Christ for sinners.

Baptism is the covenant sign of initiation. In this respect, it is for all members of the covenant community. Baptism is administered when someone formally enters the membership of the church.[4] For this reason, baptism is administered only one time. The Lord's Supper is the covenant sign of nourishment. The Lord's Supper is administered only to members of the covenant community who demonstrate the qualifications to commune with Christ by faith in the Supper. It is not administered to covenant children until and unless they meet these qualifications. Because the Supper is designed to strengthen and nourish believers in grace, it is administered frequently in the church.

The ongoing and repeated administration of the Supper in the church reminds us of an important dimension of the Lord's Supper. As wonderful as the Lord's Supper is for believers, it is not the final meal that Christ has prepared for us. That meal is the messianic banquet, the great wedding feast that Christ has prepared for his eschatological bride, the church. On that day, we will be freed from sin and woe; our bodies will be glorified, raised, and conformed to Christ's resurrection body; we will be gathered with all the elect of God; and, best of all, we will be forever in the presence of our Savior. There he will feed us in abundance with the very best of fare—himself. In the Supper, we do not have that banquet. We have tastes or appetizers of that banquet. But we should not be ungrateful. The Supper reminds us that our Savior is committed to bringing us to that banquet—he died for us on the cross to bring us near to him. And this Savior is willing, time after time, to meet with us and feed us from his Table the food that we need—the grace and benefits that are found in him alone. And the more of Christ we have in the Supper, the more we will long to be with him. And as we taste of Christ in his covenant meal again and again, we will find ourselves saying with Paul, *Maranatha*—"Our Lord, come!" (1 Cor. 16:22).

---

4. Paedobaptists understand the Scripture also to teach that the child of at least one believer is, by birthright, a member of the church and, therefore, entitled to baptism.

General Index

Scripture Index

Short Studies in Biblical
Theology Series

THE SON OF GOD
AND THE NEW CREATION

GRAEME GOLDSWORTHY

MARRIAGE
AND THE MYSTERY OF THE GOSPEL

RAY ORTLUND

WORK
AND OUR LABOR IN THE LORD

JAMES M. HAMILTON JR.

COVENANT
AND GOD'S PURPOSE FOR THE WORLD

THOMAS R. SCHREINER

THE KINGDOM OF GOD
AND THE GLORY OF THE CROSS

PATRICK SCHREINER

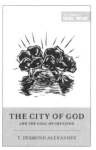

THE CITY OF GOD
AND THE GOAL OF CREATION

T. DESMOND ALEXANDER

FROM CHAOS TO COSMOS
CREATION TO NEW CREATION

SIDNEY GREIDANUS

THE LORD'S SUPPER
AS THE SIGN AND MEAL OF THE NEW COVENANT

GUY PRENTISS WATERS

For more information, visit **crossway.org/ssbt.**